Jason,

my brother. Even though its been **WAY TOO Long** since we had a chance to spend time together, your friendship is everpresent. You AnL Candice are in our prayers and there's not a day that goes by without a memory of our childhood, spent so wisely playing the never-ending whiffleball game! Thank you for sharing in so much life with me, for listening to some of my earliest sermons, for sparking some of my first theological tangents! I love you, man!

Casey

Seattle
Feb 2014

MW00974245

Trembling Love

Trembling Love

Fear, Freedom, and the God Who Is For Us

CASEY HOBBS

RESOURCE *Publications* · Eugene, Oregon

TREMBLING LOVE
Fear, Freedom, and the God Who Is for Us

Copyright © 2013 . All rights reserved. Except for brief quotations in critical publications or reviews, no part of this book may be reproduced in any manner without prior written permission from the publisher. Write: Permissions, Wipf and Stock Publishers, 199 W. 8th Ave., Suite 3, Eugene, OR 97401.

Resource Publications
An Imprint of Wipf and Stock Publishers
199 W. 8th Ave., Suite 3
Eugene, OR 97401
www.wipfandstock.com

ISBN 13: 978-1-62564-180-9
Manufactured in the U.S.A.

All scripture quotations, unless otherwise indicated, are taken from the The Holy Bible, English Standard Version® (ESV®) Copyright © 2001 by Crossway, a publishing ministry of Good News Publishers. All rights reserved. ESV Text Edition: 2011

To those who are like me: flawed, fearful, and doubting even the smallest of good news.
May God meet you along this journey.

Contents

Acknowledgments

THERE ARE NOT ADEQUATE words to thank everybody who helped along in this process. The first person that comes to mind is my big brother, Dusty. Your attention to detail in the editing process is the reason anything that follows is coherent. After that I would thank a faithful bunch of friends who took on reading and cheering me on in this process: Jay, David, and Garrett, your kind words of challenge have meant the world to me.

I should also thank the ghost of that great, however temporary community of "great and desperate sinners" at Tapestry of Hope for putting up with many of these words before they were formed into an overarching narrative. I am so proud to know men and women who can testify to the reality of a God that transforms. Thank you for allowing me to live out the gospel in community with you.

To my family: mom and dad. You have always been my biggest supporters in whatever I have taken on in life. Thank you for giving me picture after picture of what it means to have somebody who is truly *for me.*

And to Peggy: You have no idea how much your encouragement has meant to me. I can do anything you set your mind to! Thank you for the opportunity to love you, and for being patient when I fail you. I wouldn't want to take on the terrifying risks of love with anybody else.

Introduction

THAT WE ARE AFRAID is no revelation.

A few years ago, there was a commercial on television that featured a shaggy dog whose life was consumed with trouble, worry, and fear. He was so afraid that somebody would take his favorite bone away that he began looking for hiding places. He stuffed the slobbery bone under the rug, in the arm of a chair, and in a cleverly dug hole in the backyard. Finally, we see the shaggy dog depositing his bone in a bank, leaving it under lock and key. But his mind is not put at ease. He dreams about another dog slobbering all over his bone, and his sleep is interrupted, encountering insomnia, which is something that not many shaggy dogs endure over their lifetime. His fears are finally put to rest when he retrieves the bone and takes out an insurance policy. The commercial ends with an umbrella of protection over shaggy dog's precious bone. All is well with the world.

The shaggy dog's antics are a glimpse into our souls. We accept worry and fear as natural ingredients in life until we find ourselves debilitated, paralyzed with anxiety over what will come next in our unpredictable world.

What are we to do with fear? How can we survive in a world where anxiety seems to have reached its peak? How can we be expected to function with the knowledge that our proverbial bone can be taken away at any second? How can we trust a world that seems so unfair? And, more to the point, how can we trust a God who has made a world that seems to be unfair?

Two classic descriptions of God that have been expressed throughout the centuries are: "transcendence," and "immanence." In saying that God is transcendent, it is understood that he is over and above all he has made. He is, to use a word that strikes different people in different ways, sovereign. God is in charge of what he has made. He thunders when the earth quakes. He whispers in the wind. He nourishes the earth with rain and snow. God sets the ocean's limits. God upholds the universe by his power. God, in simple terms, is in charge. Another way to talk about his transcendence is that God is simply great.

But God is also immanent. He has come near. He cares about the well being of the world he has made. He is intimately involved in the world he has made to the point that he is aware of each sparrow's successful and unsuccessful flight pattern. He knows the number of hairs we have on our heads. God is with us. He is amongst us. In speaking of the immanence of God, we are simply saying that he is good.

The Christian story is full of paradox. At the center is a holy, wrathful and almighty God who displays his greatest power in his own humility. After Jesus, the one who has spoken the universe into being, and still upholds it by the word of his power, entered the world as a child in a cattle-stall, he lived a perfect life, only to take on the sin of the world, in the words of the Apostle Paul, "becoming sin for our sakes."[1] Of the common words we may use to describe the movement of God toward humanity: faith, grace, trust, obedience, love, and discipleship, the word paradox also has its place.

The faith we have inherited is an intentionally personal practice, and yet it cannot be lived out in isolation. We are warned strongly against making a public display of our faith, and yet we cannot hide it under the proverbial bushel. And while all of these seem to be contradictions, we are better off using the word paradox. We are born into a faith that is, at its core, a faith that cannot be fully explained, and yet at the same time, can only be properly lived by witnesses who have come to know that truth.

It is so tempting to skip past these paradoxical, mysterious aspects of God. Can he not just be love? Or can't he just be light? Or can he not be "the way, the truth, and the life?"[2] You see the

---

1. 2 Corinthians 5:21.
2. John 14:6.

trouble. We want to rush to defining God. We want to be free from fear, and we will allow God to try his hand in helping us, provided he can present himself as love. We are fine with God being good, in fact we prefer it that way. So we sacrifice the very thing that makes his goodness mean anything in the first place, namely, his greatness.

And who doesn't want to imagine a God who suffers with us? Who weeps with us in our pain? Who comforts us in our affliction? But if that God is not also able to stand up to injustice, then we should really change our definition of God in the first place. A "God" who is not great, who is not powerful, who does not strike fear into the hearts of his enemies, and who does not claim to have power over life and death, is not the God of the Bible. And that "God" is incapable of righting your wrongs. Taking the goodness of God and leaving the greatness of God leaves us with, at best, a cosmic shoulder to cry on. Is this someone you would be willing to trust the entirety of your life to?

But on the other hand, imagining God to be great without being good is to miss out just the same. The God of the Bible reveals himself to us as loving. He shows his care in that he would suffer with and for us. He would weep with and for us. And he would comfort us in the midst of our pain, bearing it and enter into our pain.

If we take the goodness of God and leave his greatness, we have no reason to be courageous. And if we take his greatness and leave his goodness, we have no reason to be honest.

We are in desperate need of a full picture of God. We need to know that he alone is worthy of our fear. And we need to know that he drives away our fear through his staggering goodness.

What follows is a journey through the greatness and the goodness of God.

Will you let the one who calls himself love drive your fears away, even if it is uncomfortable? I hope so. And I hope the same for myself, as well.

On a personal note, I began this project with friends in mind. I knew several men and women struggling through life–battling various addictions, suffering through grief, and searching for their place in life. One common theme I recognized in my friends was fear. There is a pathology to fear that seems to tighten its grip on people until they struggle for breath, terrified that the next moment could undo them. I began to write as something of an outsider. Sure, I could recognize a few things I was afraid of, but they would only serve as clever analogies toward my audience.

But once I started to get my thoughts down on paper, I realized that this is a book more for myself than for anybody else. For that reason, I sincerely hope that some of what follows will make sense to you. I pray that some of it will assist you in your own struggles to gain some kind of victory over fear in your own life. And I trust that whatever truth you may find is written from my perspective as a witness to the slow, sometimes surprising, oftentimes frustrating work that God is doing in me.

1

Spending Time with God

We are conditioned to be afraid.

My generation, the "MTV Generation," as we are known, has grown up with images of the Challenger's explosion, the first and second Iraqi Wars, Columbine, September 11, Virginia Tech and gigantic South Pacific tsunamis that take out nearly a half million people in one stroke. We are the kids who played video games for hours on end that had us killing terrorists. I remember my college dorm and the countless hours that were occupied with simulated violence. While we have grown up desensitized to violence, we are also the ones who have been raised to respond to the constant media shock treatments.

Is it any wonder, then, that so many of us feel like we are spinning our wheels in this life? We can so easily see what happens to people who try and fail. Better stay put and stay invisible if taking a step out into the world is as dangerous as dancing in traffic.

So many times I feel like the older brother in Jesus story about the Prodigal Son. He was watching his little brother blow it, again and again, offering no help. Something inside of him must have felt relief that somebody was worse off than he was. It must have felt good to watch his little brother come home caked in mud. He always felt good comparing his life to his brother's. What a sad, frightened man he must have been.

This cannot be the life Jesus came to give us, can it? Where is the freedom that Jesus told us he would give? Where is the friendship he offers? Have we been abandoned by Jesus and left to this half-life we are so accustomed to, or is there something better for us? We would love to agree that God is "for" us–that he is on our side–but that too seems like an empty promise.

So many of us have experienced unspeakable tragedy in our lives. So many of us look back over decades gone by and recognize our constant failure to do things the way we should. It seems there is no way God could be loving us at the same time that he allows such difficulty into our lives. God may well be good, but his love must have passed us over somewhere along the way. God may be great, but he is not on my side. He is not for me.

The gospel has become good news for other people. Over the years, history has born out the fact that priest after preacher after pastor has not really believed that what he preached was the message he needed so desperately. We may well believe that God loves sinners, but we have long ago abandoned hope that he would love us.

Have you ever felt like that? You look back over the course of twenty, thirty, or sixty years and see nothing but pain and failure. And being convinced of the futility of the past, you are afraid to look at the future. At that point, how do you find hope in the present?

I wonder how much our worlds would change if we could get a hold of the love of God for us. Could we truly be hidden from life's fears, safe in the refuge of a God who has our best interests at heart? What kind of freedom is on the other side of fear?

"Start with God–the first step in learning is bowing down to God; only fools thumb their noses at such wisdom and learning."[1]

There is an assumption in the Bible that only a fool refuses to sit in awe and wonder in the presence of the divine. Living well, it was understood, required an experiential knowledge of God. The Old Testament is full of stories about fools gaining wisdom, and about wise men becoming wiser still. Perhaps the best example is the story of Job. We meet Job as the richest man in the East. He has a wife, seven sons, three daughters, and a ton of wealth that is measured in camels, oxen, donkeys, sheep, and servants. Job had it all. Most

---

1. Prov. 1:7. Message Translation.

importantly, he was a man who "feared God and turned away from evil."[2] He was a man who was wise at the beginning of the story. And yet, by the time we reach the end, Job is a man infinitely wiser than when he started out.

Why? What happened to Job, that his wisdom so deepened? Was it the immense suffering he endured, with the loss of all ten children, along with all of his wealth? Did he learn from the advice of his friends and his wife, who all along the way pushed him toward a generic form of repentance, specifically designed to coerce God into showing mercy? What was it about Job's experience that made him a wiser man than when the story begins?

Job himself gives the answer after wrestling with God, and seeing him face to face. "I have heard of you by the hearing of the ear, but now my eye sees you; therefore I despise myself, and repent in dust and ashes."[3]

The story of Job is about a man encountering God and being changed. It is about a man struggling with his own devastating situation and asking God "why?" And it is about a man who feared God having an encounter with God. When God shows up, his grace is on display in his willingness to reveal himself as he truly is. In the end, it is the greatness of God that changes Job.

If Job was made a wiser man, a man we might say today exhibits wholeness, by encountering God, in all his greatness, I wonder if the same might happen to us today. I wonder if, in leaving out the fear of God from our common language and practice, we might be subjecting ourselves to all kinds of foolishness. That we might long ago have traded the fear of God for the fear of something less than the Almighty.

Before we go any further, it is crucial to make a distinction between the fear of God and fear of what he might do to us. The type of fear that transforms us from fools into people who can, with a small degree of accuracy, be called wise is different from a fear of consequences. The fear that might make us wise, that might transform us, is a fear that simply puts life in its proper perspective.

---

2. Job 1:1.
3. Job 42:5–6.

John Calvin once wrote that, "men (and women) are never . . . touched and impressed with a conviction of their insignificance, until they have contrasted themselves with the majesty of God."[4]

While this all might be true, it is at this point that we could really use some good news.

To be loved is to say that someone else is for us. We can depend on them. We are on their side and they are on ours. They rejoice with us and they listen to us complain. They are a safe haven amongst the dangers of life. We can be ourselves, with nothing to hide, around the ones we love. There is nothing sweeter than being in the company of those who are for us.

The message of the gospel is that God loves us. God is for us. Martin Luther wrote: "Every thought of Christ which does not begin with the assumption that God is only God for me, Christ is only Christ for me, condemns itself."[5] It is not enough just to believe God is up there in some general sense. It is not enough to cling to an abstract deity in times of need. It is not enough to have God at a distance. Our story begins with a God who is not only God, but God for us. I am still trying to wrap my mind around this thought. I think if I get a hold of it, I might look different. I might not be so afraid.

God is God for our sakes. Jesus is the God-man for us. There is great freedom available in this simple truth, though such simple truths have a way of taking a lifetime to understand.

There can be no better news than the message of the gospel–God is for us.

And that is especially good news if God is first God.

I wonder sometimes why I am more afraid of people calling to collect on student loans than I am of the living God. But I suspect that has something to do with the fact that I do not often enough encounter him.

What would change if we had the courage to meet God? Could we handle a glimpse at the backside of his glory, like Moses? And if

---

4. Calvin, *Institutes of the Christian Religion*, 39.

5. Bonhoeffer, *Christ the Center*, 47.

we came to understand just a bit of his kingship, how would such an encounter change us?

And what if, after we have paused long enough at his altar to feel our knees shaking and the earth beneath us trembling, we heard him say something so shockingly beautiful it might just change us forever?

Could we ever walk away unchanged?

2

Encountering an Earnest God

I WILL NEVER FORGET the feeling I had when I first saw the Grand Canyon. How incredibly vast and endless it was! Even as my mom hid her face when her husband and three boys took turns spitting over the edge (a must, for aspiring tourists!), I could not believe my eyes. "Grand" was such an understated term for a twelve-year-old boy looking down a mile into the center of the earth. I felt like a slight breeze might send me flying over the edge and I would fall forever. The feeling was unbelievable. It was terrifying. It drew me into the mystery of creation. That encounter was unforgettable.

Through the passing of time something has happened to my sense of wonder. I have grown up. As I think back to that first encounter with the terrible and alluring gulf, the facts are easy to access. Over the years, though, I have seen so many beautiful things that my feeling of amazement that day is only a fond memory. I have now twice driven past that great gulch without so much as stopping to stretch my legs. I am too familiar with the world to be thunderstruck at my surroundings.

If a guy named Uzzah were still with us he would be a perfect spokesman for what it means to be thunderstruck by the hand of God. Unfortunately, Uzzah is not around. He had to learn the hard way.

Uzzah grew up about nine miles away from Jerusalem, a descendent of Esau's people, and he kept noticing this large golden box with an impressive angel propped up on top of the lid. It must have seemed out of place in their home, and I bet it was at least conspicuous. But his dad had always warned him to stay away, as any good dad housing the Ark of the Covenant would naturally do. I wonder if Uzzah secretly sneaked a peek every now and again at the beautiful, majestic chest that sat in the side room. I bet he got pretty familiar with its contours, weight, and balances over the years. Almost an expert, you might say.

I have a suspicion that Uzzah felt the same way as I do about the Grand Canyon. He could remember that terrible, wonderful awe that he felt when he first saw the Ark of the Covenant. He was acutely aware that something special was housed in the two and a half cubits worth of acacia wood. Given his proximity, there are pretty good odds that he knew even more than King David "The man after God's own heart," about the golden cherubim that sat on top. He knew that the golden rings held the golden poles that ran parallel the length of the Ark, and he remembered what his father must have repeated a million times. Those poles are there so that you do not touch the Ark itself. Uzzah was familiar with the presence of God. Tragically, as we find out, Uzzah became so familiar with the Ark that he would forget about the God who inhabited it.

Well, one day, Uzzah is out in the field with his brother Ahio, when the whole of the Israelite army happens upon them. Ordinarily that would be a terrifying scene, given that Jacob and Esau's descendants did not get along all too well. But King David and his buddies were too busy dancing around in their tunics to be threatening. It was a strange sight, but Uzzah was also accustomed to strange sights. The Ark, after all, had shown up at his father's doorstep in a most unusual way, more than twenty years before.

The back-story goes that Israel was getting thrashed in a battle against the Philistines.[1] Now, for those of us unfamiliar with the history of Israel and her enemies, this shouldn't come as a surprise. The Philistines worked over Israel time and time again. It was the equivalent of a high school football team playing the Pittsburgh Steelers. Not much mystery in a victory by the army that is bigger,

---

1. 1 Sam. 5:1—6:21.

faster, stronger, and more skilled. Vegas would shut down. Nobody bets on this large of an underdog.

After 4,000 Israelites die the first day, somebody comes up with a brilliant idea. The thinking goes that God himself has defeated his people in battle through the hands of their enemies (a fact that is undisputed!). So it would be a great idea to bring the Ark of the Covenant into battle on day two. Maybe God would be bound to take into account that they had a gigantic box representing his presence, change his mind and fight for Israel. Or maybe not.

It turns out that God is not thrilled with the army's attempt to manipulate him. Day two turns out just as bad as day one, with an exception. On day two the Philistines take the Ark with them as a spoil of war.

In fact, as the prophet Samuel tells the story, it seems that the Philistines had more respect for the God represented by the Ark than did the Israelites. They fought the second day for their lives. They knew what the Lord had done to the great Egyptian army. Apparently news about a sea swallowing up a king and his army travels far and fast.

And so the Philistines carried the Ark away and set it in their god's tent. It was clear enough that their idol, Dagon, had defeated Israel's god, right? They put this mysterious, powerful, and dangerous God right next to their own statue.

Early the next morning, the priests of Dagon clock into work and notice something is amiss. Their gigantic stone statue had fallen from its perch and onto the floor. Did the temple attendants initially realize that Dagon was lying face down in front of the Ark? Who knows? I would like to say that if it were me, lifting a large stone back onto a throne, I may think twice about how, without the benefit of an earthquake, a god would find himself doing apparent homage to this mysterious box and the God it represented. But, as they say, hindsight is twenty-twenty.

Day two had to be as troubling as day one was curious. As the temple guards clock in for a day of sacrificing, they cannot help but notice that Dagon is on the ground again. This time his hands are cut off. This time his head is also cut off, lying on the floor. The lesson is clear: you may have defeated the people of God in battle (for now), but you have not reckoned on dealing with God himself. This is a living example of what the psalmist said: "Their idols are silver and gold, the work of human hands. They have mouths but do not speak; eyes, but do not see . . . they have hands but do not feel; feet, but do not walk; and they do not make a sound with their throat. Those who make them become like them; so do all who trust in them."[2]

Day two was rough. Before lunch, all of the men in the city were in desperate need of a cure for their hemorrhoid epidemic. Clearly taking the Ark was a poor decision. But how do you return the gods back to the people you have just defeated? There is no precedent for this sort of thing. Well, the priests got busy cooking up a plan to rid themselves of the divine malady. Maybe food is the way to a man's heart, but hemorrhoids are certainly an effective way to drive him to problem-solving mode.

In the years before mass-produced healing balm, the best way to get rid of this horrible scourge seemed clear: send the Ark to somebody else! "Here you go, neighbors, we have had more fun with this sacred box than we are entitled to! Your turn!" And you think re-gifting a sweater or a fruitcake is bad!

The Ark of the Covenant had three stops in Philistine territory, and all three times the Lord made the same exact point. "I am stronger than you are–you will not defeat me." Finally, the residents of the town called Ekron had enough. They came up with a strategy that, granted, sounds strange, but it was a plan nonetheless. They placed the Ark on a wagon and hitched it to two milk cows with an enclosed offering of some golden mice and some golden tumors. The tumors were for obvious reasons, and the mice represented the princes of the Philistines, who had finally understood that the God of the Ark was much, much stronger then they were. As soon as they untied the cows, the Ark was headed straight to Israelite territory, carrying along with it the curses they had suffered at the hand of God.

Back in Israelite country, the workers in a field in Beth-shemesh looked up and saw the Ark of the Lord racing in their direction. God was back on their side! As the story goes, about seventy people got too excited and looked upon the Ark. Just looked at it.

2. Ps. 115:4–8.

Keeping in mind that God has most recently inflicted his enemies with disease; he killed seventy of his friends in one fell swoop. If you think that God is not, in the words of Dietrich Bonhoeffer, "in earnest," think again. He was willing to kill seventy people for looking carelessly at the Ark of the Covenant in the middle of a celebration. You can hear the inevitable question passing their lips: "Who is able to stand before the Lord, this holy God?"

Of course, it is justifiable to be terribly afraid at this move by the Lord. The implied answer to that question is "nobody." Absolutely nobody. And so, following the lead of the Philistines, the people of God looked for somebody to pass their God off onto, like a Christmas sweater from your Aunt Hilda. To whom shall he go up away from us?

Do not run away in fear at this point. Do not explain away God's actions. Do not ignore his fury. Our Father is absolutely serious about our posture toward him.

As the story moves forward, the Ark travels to the region of Kiriath-jearim and finally to the house of Abinidab, Uzzah's father and it stayed there for two decades. And so from Israel's whining for a king and throughout entire reign of Saul, the Ark stayed in seclusion for fear that the Lord would kill more of his own people. What a troubling story, right?

Fast-forward twenty years and back to our late friend Uzzah and his brother Ahio. One day they were tending to their father's business when, all of a sudden, 30,000 soldiers, along with King David, roll up to reclaim the Ark of the Covenant. Awestruck, what choice did the brothers have but to accept the official offer to carry the Ark down to Jerusalem? Personally, I would be suspicious of an army containing–you know–soldiers, who were to a man unwilling to select two soldiers to carry the presence of God. But then again, we know more of this story than Uzzah. And again, hindsight is twenty-twenty.

As the army marched down to Jerusalem, it came time to take a rest. You know what it is like to carry furniture up and down stairs with your brother, right? He can just never hold the thing straight. As you hold your side with expert skill, your brother's lack of balance is causing the couch to constantly shifting back and forth like the Golden Gate Bridge on a gusty day. Uzzah had enough, apparently, and decided to take matters into his own hands.

After all, who is more qualified than Uzzah to grab the Ark of the Covenant if it is tipping over? He has become an expert over the years. He knows the weights and balances. He also knows that this is not just an artifact. Uzzah knew that he was handling holy business. Something must be done, and who better to act than the resident expert, right? Wrong. Just as God had done to the seventy careless worshippers twenty years prior, he immediately strikes Uzzah dead. The Lord, as it turns out, did not need Uzzah's help. Uzzah confused his familiarity with authority. The Lord once again clarified his stance. He is deadly serious when it comes to challenging his instructions.

Now, some of us show fear by flight and some show it by fight. David was a fighter, so we might think he would be likely to fight God on this one. "How could you do this to your people!" We can almost hear King David raging, pleading his cause before God, on his peoples' behalf.

But David was also terrified. Maybe keeping God at a safe distance–in this case, anyhow–wouldn't be the worst option. "How can the Ark of the Lord come to me?"[3] And so the Ark of the Covenant stays with a guy named Obed-edom.

Obed-edom is a funny sounding name. The word "Obed" means "worker," and the word "Edom" means, well, it means "Edom." If Edom sounds familiar, it is because that was Esau's nickname. This is the land that Esau worked and these are the people, many years and a few wars later, who called Esau their father. In case you are just joining us that is bad news. God hates Esau and the land that he gave him is a testament to his sentiment. The prophet Malachi describes God wrecking even his hills.[4] Obed-edom knew about working some arid, rocky soil. And he was a native Philistine to boot! Keeping with the trend of God pouring out his grace on the most unlikely, however, Obed-edom loves having the presence of God in his living room. You would too if you went from cursed to blessed in a span of three months!

3. 2 Sam. 6:9.
4. Mal. 1:3.

God blesses his enemies while his friends keep their distance. This is such a backwards story! It is only after Obed-edom sees the benefits of the presence of the Lord that David feels the safety to bring the Ark back to Jerusalem. There is something earth shattering about God loving his enemies that draws his friends back into his story.

You had better believe that King David never forgot this incident. The crazy dancing he did, including a wardrobe malfunction, was not because he no longer feared the Lord. It was because he was drawn into the presence of this God who had these immeasurably deep reservoirs of anger and grace; who could show goodness and greatness at the same time. He embraced the mystery of this highly unpredictable, yet simultaneously faithful God.

And lest we write this story off as being about somebody a long time ago, we can hear the words of Jesus echoing these terrifyingly beautiful realities. These mysterious and dangerous stories are particularly relevant for us today.

In fact, far from alleviating our fears, Jesus is the one who often stirs them up inside of us. We can deal with the God who is at a distance, crushing armies in the Ancient Near East. As long as we can place Jesus squarely in the path of this unpredictable and seemingly despotic God, we are safe. And is that not what Jesus came to do anyway? What is the cross about if it is not about appeasing the wrath of God? Can there be anything more than this to making peace with God?

At the end of the day what we are going for is neutrality. As long as our current God doesn't resemble the angry, archaic form of God in these stories, we can live with him. As long as we can get God off our backs, we are in good shape. If it takes Jesus dying for that to happen, well, so be it and thanks to Jesus. Even in our best-case scenarios we are sitting on the outside of life with God. The peace of God is about so much more.

The word Jesus brings to us is more precise: "shalom." This means not merely the absence of war, but so much more the presence of love, of fellowship, of union, and of communion. The word itself speaks of wholeness. The story of Jesus' incarnation is a one designed to bring us into the life of this God who is so often strange, disturbing, and, yes, terrifying. It was not God whose heart needed to be changed, but yours and mine. In Jesus, the Father has not changed his mind in regards to his people; he is simply extending his pursuit of us that he has started since the day we started running in the Garden.

In Matthew's telling of the life and times of the Son of God, Jesus had completed his famous "Sermon on the Mount." His syllabus has been passed out and the terms of his deal have been spelled-out in just enough detail to leave you wondering as to the details of his plan. "We get the part about meekness, blessing, patience, and all, but did you hear him say something about suffering? Or persecution? Or loving our enemies?" It was one of those great sermons that raised as many questions as it answered.

Next, Jesus heals an official's kid from an impressive distance of several miles, drives some devils into a flock of pigs, and heals a bleeding woman who touches his robe. If I am one of the apostles, I am starting to get a bit cocky. Riding with the king is a good place to be, after all, right? HBO missed their original shot at a true Entourage. Then again, their window was rather brief.

Jesus uses this opportunity to go ahead and lay out the battle plan for the coming of the new kingdom. The soldiers would travel light. They would meet with as much success as a door-to-door vacuum salesman. They would face rejection, mocking, and opposition. They would follow in the steps of Jesus and suffer at the hands of their own brothers and sisters. What would you say to your buddies to calm them down after a speech like that?

"Nothing to be afraid of people! I guarantee that the Father will be happy with you if you go through this. Just buck up, take heart, you can do it!"

Nope. Not Jesus. Again he is troubling.

"Do not fear him who can kill the body but cannot kill the soul. I will warn you who to fear: fear him who, after he has killed, has authority to cast into hell. Yes, I tell you, fear him!"[5]

Jesus came to change our minds about God not his about us. Our Father has always possessed the power to kill and the power to

5. Matt. 10:28.

bring life. The story of Jesus is simply a continuation of the authority of his Father playing out in the world. That is why he can say something so serious. He knows that the way to freedom is obedience. In a startling turn of events, freedom is found in fear.

Do you see what Jesus is doing here? He is liberating us from the crippling effects of misplaced fear. God is the one to take seriously. Our Father is the one who calls the shots. He is calling us away from the dread of failure. God alone is judge. The way to comfort is simply by re-arriving at a fear of God.

We have done ourselves no favors by reshaping God into our own image. We want God to be easy-going. We want him to be accepting. We want him to be happily ignorant of our flaws. We want the lion but not the teeth. We want the fire but not the heat. We want to be forgiven without the relationship. Here again, Jesus is troubling.

The question becomes whether or not we are willing to live life with a God who has the authority to kill and cast away from his presence. Are we looking for a god we can manipulate to do our will or are we looking for a God who commands us to do his? Paraphrasing Martin Luther, "Are we forced to make God good or are we willing to let God be God?"

And herein lies the warning for those of us who have become experts in the things of God. Our Father is entirely serious. He asks us for our whole heart, if we would be free from fear. We, who know about God like we know about the back of our hand, are in deep, dire danger of falling into the same fate as Uzzah. We no longer lack for factual data and doctrinal depth but for that feeling of fear, dread, and awe in the presence of God.

The writer of Hebrews warns us to be wise and check ourselves. The proper response to a God as great and powerful as the one in the Bible is trembling love. The longer we sit with this God, the more we become aware that our lives are constantly in his hands.

"Therefore let us be grateful for receiving a kingdom that cannot be shaken, and let us offer to God acceptable worship, with reverence and awe, for our God is a consuming fire."[6]

6. Heb. 12:28–29.

It is not too late for us to learn Uzzah's lesson. We are not yet too proud to stop and tremble in the presence of the Almighty. This God who is for us is wild, free, powerful, and best described as an unquenchable fire.

If we want freedom from the fear of the trivial we must embrace the fear of the Living God.

3

Waiting on Jesus

A FRIEND ONCE ASKED me to share about praying through the Psalms in his Wednesday night group. This is something that believers have been doing for centuries and I have personally found it very helpful in nourishing my spiritual life day by day. And so I shared with the group how I have been strengthened by praying through the psalms and encouraged them to do the same, taking one psalm in the morning and one in the evening.

I was introduced to praying the Psalms through the writings of Dietrich Bonhoeffer. His premise was that the entire Bible pointed to Jesus, the second person of the Triune God. Each story, song, poem, and genealogy both points forward, to, or back at the incarnation, death, descent to hell, resurrection, ascension, mediation (Jesus' ongoing work of prayer for us) and promised second coming of the Son of God. Bonhoeffer was not alone in this view. He had received it from his prime source, Martin Luther, who has routinely been accused of finding Jesus "under every rock and stone." Bonhoeffer, in keeping with his long-deceased mentor, would take such an accusation as a compliment.

Bonhoeffer's belief was that each of the 150 entries of the Psalms was the prayer of Jesus himself. The Son of God is the primary petitioner of every Psalm, so when King David pleads his innocence before the Lord (which seems outrageous!) with statements such as, "The Lord dealt with me by my merit, for the cleanness of my hands, he requited me,"[1] David can only be praying this through the innocence of the perfect Son of God. Likewise, when he repents of his outrageous deeds (say, for instance, impregnating his soldiers' wife while he was away at war, then having him killed), David can cry out: "Have mercy on me, O God, according to your steadfast love; according to your abundant mercy blot out my transgressions!"[2] The only way he can have a prayer that his wickedness will be forgiven is through the person and work of his great and coming descendent, Jesus. Only if Jesus prays these words on his account can David have a hope of them being heard before the Lord.

On Friday morning I got a phone call from another friend who had heard me share and taken the advice to heart. Thursday morning, he woke up and prayed Psalm 1: "Blessed is the man who doesn't walk in the way of the wicked . . . but his delight is in the law of the Lord."[3] His whole day was changed, renewed and whole as he reflected the smiles of Christ upon him, not only in his time of meditation, but throughout his entire day. Day one was a success.

Then came Friday. His comfort was turned to dismay as he prayed Psalm 2: "Kiss the Son, lest he be angry and you perish in the way."[4]

Now, even if you were reading the psalms without looking for Jesus, there he is, right? Who else in the Bible can be the capital "S" Son? Remembering my advice to see Christ himself in each psalm, my friend's comfort turned to alarm.

I thought that Jesus loved me!

I thought that God was not angry at me!

I thought that God was for me!

But here is Jesus, plain as the nose on your face, in Psalm 2, asking for the nations as his "inheritance." Oh, that's so nice, Jesus is going to take us heathens, and pursue us with his love! That is fantastic! But then you see very quickly why Jesus wants the nations.

1. Ps.18:21.
2. Ps. 51:1.
3. Ps. 1:1.
4. Ps. 2:1.

Here is Jesus, clear as daylight, desiring to smash the nations up like a clay pot![5]

And there is more. Can you imagine a God who mocks people? If I were writing this psalm, I would not have included a Father/Son laugh-fest at the expense of even the most evil realms of humanity. It seems like God should be above all this. Does God not have anything better to do than sit in heaven and mock his enemies?

How can this be the same Jesus we have become accustomed to seeing raising the dead and preaching peace?

And there is the real problem, right? God, we are told in the Sermon on the Mount, "loves his enemies."[6] It just does not seem right that Jesus would be presenting himself in this vindictive light. He is the one who, "while we were still sinners…died for us!"[7] We were enemies and Jesus: "made peace by the blood of his cross."[8]

Jesus mocks his enemies.

Jesus loves his enemies.

This message just will not sell.

At the end of the day, we have two choices when we come to these things that seem to be wild contradictions in the nature of God. We can either stand in judgment over Scripture, or we can take God at his word. Here again we are confronted with that apparent contradiction that our spiritual grandparents called "mystery," and "paradox."

There is a story that the disciple Matthew told about a Canaanite woman whose daughter was oppressed by some evil spirits. How they had been oppressing her, what her mother had tried and how long the struggle had plagued the young girl, we do not know. What we do know is that she had heard about a healer who was capable and willing to heal diseases, cast out demons, bind up the wounded, and bring freedom to the spiritual slaves. She had to think that, if given an audience with this strange, healing teacher, she might just get her daughter back, after all.

5. Ps. 2:9.
6. Matt. 5:44.
7. Rom. 5:6.
8. Eph. 1:20.

And so, as Jesus, the man who was God, roams around the countryside healing and teaching, the Canaanite woman somehow obtains of his speaking schedule, which, in the days before Twitter updates, Facebook updates, and email blasts is impressive in and of itself. Then she approaches the God-man with all the humility and terror of an outsider yet all the faith of a child. Did I mention she was an outsider?

The Canaanites had the unfortunate role in history as those people who originally lived in the land that we would call today "Israel," on the far side of the Jordan River. Way back in the story of the Exodus, Moses and his successors Joshua and Caleb headed to Canaan, which was also known as the "Promised Land." The Canaanites, as you may well imagine, were never too keen on the idea of surrendering their land, giving up their gods and living under the reign of a new people and their all-powerful God. Word had also been spread in the forty years of Israel's trek from Egypt to Jericho that Israel's God was the one who swallowed up the entire Egyptian army, Pharaoh and all. It makes pretty good sense that the Canaanites fought the haggard band of Israelites who claimed divine rite to the land their fathers worked, right?

What they could not know was that God had already made a promise that he would drive out the inhabitants from the land he had chosen for his people. It has been well established by now that the God of the Bible is the one whose plan wins out without fail.

If you want to read about the battles of the Canaanites to keep the land, you can read all about it in the book of Joshua. Long story short, God won and the people drove out the Canaanites from the land of Canaan. Is it only me, or does that seem more than a little unfair?

Suffice to say that over the ensuing centuries from Joshua to Jesus, you would not want to be a Canaanite in Jerusalem. If you want to step into her shoes, read the prophets when they talk about the regions of Tyre and Sidon. Read about the heaps of fire and brimstone that are spent on the remaining Canaanites. But the woman in Jesus' story had bigger fish to fry. Remember, she had a daughter who was slipping away into the clutches of hell itself.

So with all the boldness it must have required, this woman comes to the Maker of heaven and earth and cries out to Jesus, calling him "Lord, son of David "(a Canaanite calling out to the king of the Jews!), and pleading with him: My daughter is severely oppressed by a demon.[9] She is not asking for an explanation of the past centuries of hardships for her people. She lays aside her shame, her fears, and her pride to ask the king of heaven to relocate a few demons. She is certainly asking nothing outside Jesus' realm of expertise.

How might you expect Jesus to answer the woman? Maybe he asks to see the daughter so he can speak directly to this harmful spirit. Maybe he embraces the woman, shattering all cultural barriers, and assuring her of deliverance. Maybe he answers her with a parable and a promise to drive out all evil from the face of the earth one day, starting with her daughter. Jesus is a hard one to figure, but we can almost feel the healing power that is coming from his voice as we read the story. And then this:

"But he did not answer her a word."[10]

Have you ever felt like Jesus is intentionally looking the other way? Honestly? Have you ever felt like Jesus was flat-out ignoring your pleas for help? Our worst fears in these darkest of hours became reality for this poor woman. Jesus turned a deaf ear.

And maybe, just maybe, in those times when you feel Jesus refuses to hear you, you press on and keep wrestling, like Jacob did so long ago with the Angel of the Lord. In your spiritual tenacity you cry out, "I will not let you go without a blessing!" On our best days we trust in the good heart of Jesus even when we hear no answer from his lips. And that is exactly what this woman did. She stayed in the conversation. She had to know that this would be her daughter's last and only chance. If God in the flesh could not hear her cries, she would just have to beg.

And beg she did. So much begging, in fact, that the disciples came up to Jesus and pleaded her case. It was bad press to have a poor, sincere, helpless woman begging with no response from the

---

9. Matt. 15:22.
10. Matt. 15:23.

Great Physician. But Jesus made his case clear to his followers. "I was sent only to the lost sheep of the house of Israel."[11] The message is clear. She was a member of a sorry bunch of people who had opposed God's plan so many years ago. Jesus came for his own people. He had not come for her.

Does this seem unnerving to anybody else? Jesus is the one who came to save his people from their sins, to heal the sick, to raise the dead, and to announce God's plan coming to fruition on earth, and here he is ignoring a desperate, pleading woman just because she comes from the wrong neighborhood. Jesus is supposed to be on our side. He is supposed to champion the disenfranchised and here he is, unwilling to help this poor woman and her demon-possessed daughter. I wonder if she was as surprised as I am by the silence of God standing right in front of her.

She may have been surprised but she did not miss a beat. She fell down at the feet of the almighty and begged him with those simple, trusting words that only humble lips can utter: "Lord help me."

And as if Jesus' first two responses were not harsh enough, on the third request he dropped the proverbial hammer. "It is not right to take the children's bread and throw it to the dogs."[12]

Now, we can stop the story right here. What would you do if you were in the Canaanite woman's place? Would you run? Would you fight? Would you be repulsed? What happens when an encounter with the Son of God does not go your way? What happens when your prayers are answered with a firm "no?" What happens when your expectations are shattered? What happens when you find out that Jesus does not play to your expectations?

Would he be worth listening to even if it seemed he was against you?

The 1968 novel by Charles Portis, True Grit, which inspired John Wayne's only Academy Award in its subsequent movie version, and a 2010 re-make tells the same gripping story of Mattie, a girl at the age of fourteen, who is avenging her father's murderer. As the story unfolds, we find that the murderer is part of Lucky Ned

11. Matt. 15:24.
12. Matt. 15:26.

Pepper's gang. Mattie recruits Marshall Rooster Cogburn and Texas Ranger LaBoeuf and they seek out Pepper's gang for vengeance. After days of riding through the unforgiving Oklahoma terrain, the motley band of a proud Texas Ranger, a drunken vagabond lawman, and a girl after revenge happen upon Lucky Ned and his gang.

In the course of the action, Lucky Ned Pepper's gang captures Mattie and holds her for ransom while the outlaws plot their escape from the Marshall and the Ranger.

As Ned begins to assess his options, asking Mattie to make sense of the situation, the little girl looks for a way out of the situation. It is not Lucky Ned Pepper that she has come for after all. She would be satisfied even with the ringleader's escape, so long as her father's murderer is brought to justice. As she has done over and over in the story, she offers the help of her brilliant lawyer, who would surely stand up for even Lucky Ned, on her behalf, in court. She asked the outlaw, "Do you need a good lawyer?"

It sure sounds like Lucky Ned Pepper needed a good lawyer. And so do we. And so did the Canaanite woman.

How can you read the account of the Canaanite woman's encounter with the living God without wanting to stick up for her? She does not have any kind of advocate in this situation. Nobody is speaking up for her. And it makes you wonder how long she had been alone in her struggles. Who would possess the credentials to stand up in the presence of the divine and plead her case? What happens when Jesus refuses to take up for her? What happens when it feels he does the same to you? You look to God for justice and you come home empty handed. Are you disgusted with God, or worse, are you ready to disregard him? Are you ready to file a lawsuit in God's court?

Lucky for Lucky Ned that he was a bit more perceptive than your average outlaw. He realized he had no case, even if he assembled an Old West "Dream Team" of lawyers. It would not be enough for somebody to make a good case for him. He needed more, so he stated his need a bit more precisely: "I need a good judge."[13] And so do we. And so did the Canaanite woman.

13. Portis, *True Grit*, 235.

The problem with all this, though, is that Jesus calls himself judge.[14] What happens when the judge renders a verdict that cuts against you? What if his judgment jars you? What if his ruling seems unjust? It seems like Jesus came to fix this issue, right? That he came to soothe us; to keep us from all harm and pain; to be on our side.

How can God be for us and against us at the same time? How can he be fighting for us when it feels like he is only fighting against us?

These seemingly polar opposite truths bring us to an immediate crossroads. If we stand in judgment over the word of God we have become those kings, those rulers, those nations, those peoples at the beginning of Psalm 2. Can you imagine humanity working to knock God off his throne? What if the three branches of the United States government decided they were fed up and set out to reject the rule of God? Or what if the United Nations came up with the same idea and the world was to unite in one plan to "off" God? Would every man, woman, and child on the face of the earth, united in war against God stand a chance? Really? Is there anything more ridiculous than humanity trying to take God's place as sovereign ruler?

And what about the Canaanite woman? What do you expect her to do, when God himself speaks harshly to her? Does she cower in fear? Does she run for cover? Does she fight against the healer whose favor she so desperately needs? Most likely our answer to these questions tell us more about ourselves than anything else.

Me? I would run. I would like to say I would have the strength of will to even fight against Jesus here but, if I am being honest, I would be out of there before you could say the word "coward." I can picture myself, walking back home empty-handed. No cure for my ailing daughter. As I kicked up the dust underneath my feet, I would come up with something clever to say when I walked in the house. Sorry, God hates us, I did what I could but I guess we had it coming for one reason or another.

And whether it was her deep well of faith, her diminished mental state caused by taking care of a demon-possessed daughter, her sheer desperation, or a combination of the three; the true shock to the story comes in the fact that she stays. She has thought about

14. Jn. 5:27.

what she might say to God, if she–a woman from Tyre and Sidon–were ever given such a chance. What did she say?

"Yes, Lord, yet even the dogs eat the crumbs that fall from their masters' table."[15]

No defense. No seeking after a lawyer. No offence taken. She does not make her case based on merit but on grace. What kind of a master does not feed his dog? Even if she was a dog, she still had some provision, some love, some rain, some sun, and most importantly, some healing coming her way. She does not run away when the loving Jesus appears grouchy. He does not have to live up to her expectations. She has nowhere else to go.

So the question becomes, does Jesus have to live up to our expectations? What if he gives us an answer we do not like? What if the love of Jesus upsets our world? What if the presence of Christ causes us to re-think our positions in life? Will we be like the Canaanite woman? Will we wait for him to love us on his own terms? Will we have even the clarity of Ned Pepper, who has given up on making a defense against the court? Or will we resist–or worse–run and hide like Adam and Eve in the Garden of Eden, trembling in fear that God, in his justice, will find us out.

Make no mistake. This is exactly what each of us has done every day of our lives.

Instead of submitting to God's rule, we have worked to build our own kingdoms. We have set up a puppet rule of sex, drugs, work, family, relationships, and a million other things–both good and bad–to keep command of our personal marionette. This is a ridiculous position. As long as we insist on running things our way, even bringing God's word under our judgment, we have set ourselves up against him. We will lose that fight.

The Canaanite woman came to Jesus with empty hands. She came with no contingency plan. She came seeking the relief of justice that only the Judge of the whole earth could grant her.

And, at last, Jesus gave her mercy. Blown away by her faith, Jesus does what we have been expecting him to do all along. He

---

15. Matt. 15:27.

speaks the word and the poor woman's daughter was free for the first time in who knows how long.

What would you do if Jesus turned out to be more unpredictable, if he had more of an edge, than you had once imagined? What if he was in the habit of doing things in his own way, in his own time?

Would you still call him King?

Would you still call him Judge?

Would you still wait for him to come through?

Could you still trust him?

4

A Wild Spirit

I HAVE TO BE honest and say that I cannot remember the last time I felt fear for the Holy Spirit.

Then again, I have to rack my brain to come up with the last conversation about the Holy Spirit that did not start off something like this: "I know it sounds crazy to quit my job and join the circus, but I just feel like the Holy Spirit is telling me to take a risk." Or maybe something resembling this: "Well, I know you feel like you are not a horrible person for skipping prayer meeting to have a drink with your friends after work but I will just be praying that the Holy Spirit points out what a sinner you are, dude."

Is the Holy Spirit essentially the "genie" person of the Trinity, who, when released, will grant as many as three wishes at a time . . . three, of course, being the number of persons in the Trinity, and days in Memorial Day weekend? Or is the Holy Spirit the agent of God that snoops around our (friends') business and points out our (their) mistakes? Either way, for some reason we forget about the Holy Spirit, who Jesus was so interested in introducing to his disciples.

And if we have completely forgotten about the Holy Spirit, what sense does it make to be afraid of him? It seems a whole lot more convenient to just forget about him, and move on to more pertinent topics, like politics, or the newest reality television show. Still, if we are interested in knowing God as he has shown himself, it would do us some good to sit with this odd-man-out in the Trinity.

And that is what he is, right? Even if we go out of our way to remind ourselves that the Spirit is a "he–meaning that he possesses person-hood–not an it," we still lack a good category for him. We have a category for understanding or misunderstanding the relationship of Father and Son, but Son to Spirit?

I can only speak for myself, but the only friendly ghost I knew growing up was Casper; and I was never afraid of Casper. One more time, it seems as if the Lord has a way of shattering the old catego-ries we have been operating with all this time.

Jesus told his disciples, the night he was arrested, that he was leaving them.[1] He told them that things were going to change dra-matically. When they woke up, they would no longer be subject to the usually bizarre travel itinerary and equally weird daily to-do list. No more fishing trips to find coins with Caesar's face. No more aquatic strolls. No more quick exits from hometowns to make a beeline to death. No more hungry crowds to feed with rations that would not feed the Brady Bunch. The Master was going away. The mentor was going to die. The teacher was going to leave his pupils to figure out the life he would provide them with by his blood; but it would turn out all right. He would not forget them. He would send the Holy Spirit.

Honestly, if I am hearing this for the first time, I am with the oft-maligned and so-called "Doubting" Thomas, I kinda doubt this is going to end well. Unseen ghosts on order are rarely of great com-fort to the grieving community.

Fast-forward forty days. Jesus has died, descended into hell, and risen from the dead. He spends that month rolling around his old stomping grounds, holding out his hands and side to skeptics, just like Thomas. Skeptics like me. Then he tells his friends to stay in Jerusalem and wait. For the authorities to find them? Nope. He tells them to wait for the Holy Spirit. You have to think that the death and resurrection of Jesus helped them take a bit more comfort in this promise the second time, but how much hope can you possibly have in a promise you cannot even begin to comprehend?

---

1. Jn. 16:5–15.

The disciples have more faith than I do, so they go to Jerusalem and wait; and it is a good thing, too, because not long after that, they were dramatically surrounded and dressed in the power of God, just like Jesus said they would be. And the church was born. Peter gives a sermon on the life, death, burial, resurrection, and ascension of the God-man. The Holy Spirit shows up and translates the language of the sermon so that the most common foreigner could understand. The church effectively expanded from twelve cowards into 3,012 men and women who had finally experienced the first tastes of the life Jesus had been proclaiming for the last three years. Everything changed.

When Jesus died, he left his mother, Mary Magdalene, John the Apostle, and some other lady named Mary. Not much of an obituary: Deceased: Carpenter, Rogue, God-in-Flesh; Age 33; Survived by his mom, two women with whom he had a platonic relationship, and John, a man inconsequential enough to identify himself with an executed insurgent without showing up on the radar of the authorities. For all the admirers Jesus gained, it seems he had very few followers at the time of his death.

And followers were what Jesus came to win, not admirers. Nineteenth-century philosopher Søren Kierkegaard pointed out the difference between an admirer and a follower: "What then, is the difference between an admirer and a follower? A follower is or strives to be what he admires. An admirer, however, keeps himself personally detached. He fails to see that what is admired involves a claim upon him, and thus he fails to be or strive to be what he admires."[2] What a disappointment, then, when, at Jesus' most vulnerable moment, the closest thing he has to followers look more like those who appreciate his work from a distance! When the Holy Spirit came, though, he won a people who would put their lives on the line for the gospel.

And here is Peter–the guy whose dedication at the arrest of Jesus ranged from ridiculous attempted murder to inexcusable spinelessness culminating in cutting all ties with his best friend–multiplying the followers of Jesus 251 times in the span of one page in our Bibles.

---

2. Kierkegaard, *Bread and Wine*, 56.

What caused such a drastic change? Luke, the writer of the book of Acts, lets us in on the secret: the Holy Spirit has arrived in a big way. Now, to say he had just arrived is a bit misleading because he had been there all along. When God created the heavens and the earth, the Spirit hovered over the water.[3] When the prophet Samuel, anointed Saul, he promised him that the Spirit would rush onto him at just the right time;[4] but when he turned his back on God, the Holy Spirit left Saul.[5] When Gabriel told Mary that she would have a child, he mentioned that the Holy Spirit would work in her to bring about the virgin pregnancy.[6] And when Jesus came out of the water of baptism, the Holy Spirit was there, as a dove, joining with the Father in the celebration for Jesus' obedience on our behalf.[7] The Holy Spirit had been there all along, working behind the scenes, but always present.

He has always been there, but in those first days of the church, the Holy Spirit takes center-stage. He reminds Jesus' followers about the words he told them. He convicts the converts about their self-centered ways and he compelled the church to love the less fortunate in their community. This was a sort-of-golden age for the church. Everybody shared their possessions; nobody going hungry. Everybody was experiencing the life that Jesus laid out in the beatitudes. How could you not like the Holy Spirit, right? And then there was Ananias and his wife Sapphira. Aren't some stories better off left untold?

And yet, there it is in plain old black and white: a terrifying story that seems out of place. If it happened way back in the Old Testament, we might be able to put Jesus in the way. Well, since Jesus came, things are different. God no longer punishes sin. For sure, that is what I want to say. The problem is that the story is still there. And the characters are not all that unfamiliar to us today.

3. Gen. 1:2.
4. 1 Sam. 10:6.
5. 1 Sam. 16:14.
6. Lk. 1:35.
7. Jn. 1:32.

Against the backdrop of this incredible giving campaign for those who were in need steps in a despicable couple of ingrates, a dude named Ananias, and his wife Sapphira. Following suit with the others, they also sold their property and gave to the church.[8] The story became news worth reporting when they sat down, schemed, tight-wadded, and devised a plan to rip off the body of Christ. By now you may have guessed it. They sold their house and gave, in Luke's words, "only a part" of it to the Apostles to distribute among the needy. Can you imagine the selfishness? What do you think they did with the other part of the money? Did they double-down on a camel at the tracks? Did they buy a ton of Tupperware in efforts to sell it to their unsuspecting friends at church?

As the story unfolds, Ananias rolls into the congregation with bags full of money and presents them proudly at the feet of the disciples. Now, you may remember in Sunday school hearing about the dangers of public contributions. Did Jesus not say something about your right hand not knowing what your left hand was doing? Thinking he could outwit the God who had given him his wits in the first place though, Ananias fudged the numbers. He proudly announced that every dime of their house was now in the offering plate. He had not banked on the Holy Spirit telling Peter exactly how much the home had sold for, however.

And so, right away, Peter levies the charge: "why has Satan filled your heart to lie to the Holy Spirit?"[9] He makes it absolutely clear that the issue is deeper than a couple making some money on the sale of a house. They were never required to give every dime to the church. They were never required to sell their house. Instead, they had written their own law and, in efforts to impress their friends, they had made a pact to lie to God himself.

Out of nowhere, the Holy Spirit strikes Ananias dead on the spot. And the worship service goes on.

A few hours go by and Sapphira enters the room. When Peter asked Sapphira for details, she made it all too obvious that husband

---

8. Acts 5:1–2.
9. Acts 5:3.

and wife had decided to pull a fast one. Again, how would you expect the Holy Spirit to react to this bold-faced lying?

Sapphira, like her husband, is struck dead on the spot.

How would you expect the Holy Spirit to react to the posing of Ananias and Sapphira? It is important to remember that the real dishonesty is in the fact that they had agreed to lie about their gift. Everybody else was giving so much, it seemed they had to keep pace. Who knows if we would know their names today if they stood up boldly and said: "Here is eighty percent of our profit for the sale of our home!"

How could they expect Jesus' promised Comforter to kill them on the spot? Can you imagine that? Does that trouble you? Does that give you pause? Does that strike fear into your heart? I know that this whole story terrifies me. And do you know whom else it terrified? Everybody. Luke wrote: "And great fear came upon all who heard of it."[10]

If you were writing a story about God's lovingly reckless, radical, and finally effectual pursuit of his rebellious creation, would you include this episode? Would you tell all about the time some cheapskate and his wife were struck dead on site? After swinging the public tide and headed on a meteoric rise, would you break out and kill a few stragglers? Would you jeopardize your momentum like that? No way I would. But then again, that just may be the point.

The Holy Spirit is not like us. He's not like us at all. He has his own agenda and he does not need our strategic advice in one iota of its execution. This too, terrifies us.

Jesus' best friend, John, compared the Spirit to unquantifiable, vast and sometimes-devastating things like "wind," "water," and "fire." These are not the type of elements we cozy up to. They are the type of things we buy insurance to protect ourselves from. I wonder if there were any opportunistic entrepreneurs running around selling Spirit insurance after the untimely death of Ananias and Sapphira.

Today, it seems as if we cannot turn around without a well-meaning preacher pedaling protection from the unexpected. Who

10. Acts 5:5.

is the most effectual preacher you have ever heard? The one who gets to your emotions, mind, and will as soon as he or she starts the sermon?

It may sound terribly arrogant, but if I can be gut honest for a second, I would say that my heart is my most effectual preacher. He tells me to play it safe. He tells me to run away from painful relationships. He tells me to slack off at work. He tells me to give up on my dreams. He tells me that my life is too important to hand over to any Ghost: friendly, fearsome, or holy. My heart pedals protection from the unexpected on a daily basis. And he is getting wilier with age. Each time I listen to my heart I choose to insulate myself from the wild and life inducing movement of God.

A thousand times a day I am faced with two choices. I can trust my twisted, panicking, fearful heart or I could trust this mysterious, thunderous, unpredictable Spirit who offers me freedom. The questions boil down over and over again to the one question: "will I fear God or will I fear everything else?" The choice, again and again, is between fear and freedom.

Ok, so back to the story of Ananias and Sapphira. Can you see yourself in this faithless couple? Have you ever cooked the books or are you the last honest person alive? Have you ever lived your life to please others? Have you ever lied to gain acceptance or am I alone?

All along, we are much more willing to risk upsetting the Spirit of God than we are to risk upsetting our husband, our wife, our roommate, our boss, our friends, or our children. Are we so afraid of being alone that we are willing to lie straight to the face of God? Are we so paralyzed in terror of the people and situations around us that we have forgotten the God who calls himself wind, water, and fire?

The Greek word that we translate as Spirit is the same word we translate in other places as wind. In Jesus' discussion with Nicodemus[11], he plays off this double meaning. You can hear where the wind is blowing but who knows where it is coming from or where it is going? The wind is going to blow where the wind wants to blow and that is that. That is what we call freedom. And do you

11. Jn. 3:8.

know what? Jesus told Nicodemus that we have that same freedom. So it is with everyone who is born of the Spirit. That terrifying and magnetic freedom that the Spirit possesses is what he is working in us as he is making us new moment-by-moment. No wonder Martin Luther could say, "bewilderment is the true comprehension."[12] He was being made new by the Spirit. His fear of the unknown was dying away; Luther was experiencing true freedom.

Almost a year before Jesus was executed for his crimes against the comforts of the powers that be, he stood up in the middle of a feast and made a startling statement. Jesus stood up in the middle of the Feast of Booths and said, If anyone thirsts, let him come to me and drink. Whoever believes in me, as the Scripture has said, "Out of his heart will flow rivers of living water". As John wrote about this strange scene, he shed some light on the situation. "Now this he said about the Spirit . . ."[13] The Spirit nourishes, but he is on his own program. He nourishes like a river flows- constant, steady, powerful, and dangerous. And do you see how he calls us again to participation? The tides may very well rise up and carry our care-fully constructed lives downstream. The Spirit, like a rushing river, has a way of keeping us alive, even if sometimes that means that the river swells and washes away our safe-havens.

Do you remember John the Baptizer's message? "I baptize you with water but he who is mightier than I is coming . . . He will baptize you with the Holy Spirit and with fire."[14] The Spirit is the one who would come and separate the proverbial wheat and chaff. He would tend the garden and toss the weeds on top of the fire. The Spirit comes to destroy the enemies of his people, just as a good farmer cares for his crop. He means to give us space to grow, to be nourished and to be free from predators. The fire of the Spirit is all grace. The Spirit is fire for us, purging us of the weeds that otherwise would choke the life out of us.

It is time for us to take stock of the God we are dealing with. Are we willing to hand over our will and lives over to God, even

12. Dietrich Bonhoeffer, *The Cost of Discipleship*. (New York: Touchstone, 1995), 93.

13. John 7:37–39.

14. Luke 3:16.

when he tells us that we have every reason to tremble in his presence? Even when he tells us that he is as unpredictable as the wind? Even when he tells us that he is as powerful as a river? Even when he tells us that he is as serious and threatening as fire? When our hearts preach a message of insecurity, and fear will we let the Spirit counter our fears? Will we let him overwhelm our fears? Will we let him call us into this way of true freedom, even if it will cost us every safe haven we have spent our lives building?

Your answer may be "no." You may want to run and hide from such a wild, unpredictable God, but only take one word of caution: be prepared to be afraid of each and every situation, person, thought, feeling, hurt, joy, and experience you will ever have. Only a God who is to be feared above all else could possibly handle your fear of rejection, failure, and abandonment.

The good news is that he is not only powerful enough to capture us in fear, but he is humble enough to captivate us in love. God does the unthinkable. He comes down to us. He comes down to be one of us. He comes down to live for us; to die for us; to take on hell for us; to raise to new life for us; to ascend into heaven for us; to pray for us; to prepare a place for us; to prepare us for a place; to guide us; to return for us; and to live with us in true, unbound freedom.

How could such a terrifying God be totally compassionate and worthy of not only adoration, but also, emulation? Do not be afraid. There is more. There is so much more.

5

Fearless Love?

"THERE IS NO FEAR in love, but perfect love casts out fear. For fear has to do with punishment, and whoever fears has not been perfected in love."[1]

It is not enough to admit our fear of God. A grace that teaches us to fear and then leaves us alone only brings us knowledge. It does not bring us freedom and it does not bring us love. It only brings fear. And fear only brings us to the starting line. It brings our knowledge of God up to par with the demons. Even they confess God and tremble. Their deficiency does not lie in knowledge, or a lack of fear. It lies in the absence of love.

I have found that I have a much easier time being afraid of God than I do loving him with all of my heart, all of my mind, and all of my strength. How do we make this transition from a people paralyzed by fear to a people free to love God and neighbor? What is our turning point?

The easy answer, the one I come up with first, is to point to the coming of the Holy Spirit.

I think about Peter, one of Jesus' best friends. I have always identified with Peter, and I have always assumed that it was because he was so impulsive. Peter was the kind of guy who was liable to say or do anything. He corrected Jesus when he heard the eternal plan

---

1. 1 Jn. 4.18.

of God laid out for the first time.[2] Imagine the arrogance of trying to set the guy you have just admitted was God straight! And when the soldiers came to arrest Jesus, it was Peter who drew his sword and sliced off the ear of the servant of the High Priest.[3] Peter seems wild, he seems impulsive, and he seems brave.

But then, once Jesus heals the servant's ear and submits himself to the authorities, we get a more accurate picture of Peter. We find out that Peter is a coward. After all, it was Peter who denied any association with the man he believed to be God. Three times, he sold his soul for nothing but fear.[4] And we start to see him differently.

Why did Peter correct Jesus as he laid out the grand plan? Was he so committed to his friend that he could not bear the thought of his torture? Or was he secretly afraid of what might happen to him if his teacher died? Maybe he had been looking for a way out of his life of tending nets and he could see his dreams of grandeur fading away. He would become a nobody once again, trapped in his boat like a fish in a net. This was his chance to rise above his circumstances, after all, and here is his fearless leader leading him to the cross. Peter is afraid.

And was it courage that compelled Peter to draw his sword? He was more than happy to make the High Priest's servant suffer, but where was he when Jesus went to trial? Peter was nowhere to be found. What a coward.

But Peter's story takes a dramatic turn when the Holy Spirit shows up, speaking through him with power, authority, and fire. Peter himself is arrested, questioned, beaten, and yet he shows himself to be the rock that Jesus called him to be.[5] The coming of the Holy Spirit changed his life forever.

So the correct answer is that we need the power of the Holy Spirit to be fearless leaders in the church.

But for as long as I have had the Spirit of God making his dwelling place in my heart, sometimes it seems like I am no less

2. Mk. 8:32.
3. Jn. 18:10.
4. Jn. 18:15–18; 25–27.
5. Matt. 16:18.

afraid than when I first started out. And it makes me wonder more about Peter. I mean, if all he needed was to be Spirit-filled to be free from fear, then it seems like I missed the boat. And that makes me, well, afraid. But what if Peter was only a different man incrementally? That is to say, what if he became a new man piece by piece?

After all, that was what Peter's friend John meant when he wrote a letter addressing fear. He said that perfect love casts out fear. This word, perfect, means something slightly different than when we say it.

What we mean by perfect is that there is no mistake whatsoever. A woman with perfect skin has no blemishes. A pugilist with a perfect record has not been beaten in a fight. A pitcher with a perfect game set down each batter he faced. Perfect, to us, is akin to flawless, and while this is in the same ballpark as John's meaning, he is not talking about flawless love. He is talking about completed love. Small difference, but in that case, John is making a whole lot more sense.

John is telling us that love has a way of progressively ridding us of fear.

There is a slow, incremental change that comes upon us as we let love change us. To me, that is comforting, because sometimes it seems like I am miles behind.

I remember being a freshman in high school, at the end of August, just before the school year began, trying out for the soccer team. As I looked around, I sized up the other kids to see how I stacked up. Soccer was never my sport, but I had to stay in shape somehow before baseball season in the spring, and my big brother was a fixture on the team entering his senior year. So I figured I'd give it a shot.

The only other player I knew was my twin brother, and he was the only guy on the field who did not tower over me. But the one thing I had going for me was speed. My hopes for following in my big brother's footsteps were banked on out-running the others. And even that stood in jeopardy as soon as the day started.

We started the tryout by running around the track a couple of times. As soon as we were off, one of the other boys took off like he was shot out of a cannon. That was it. First five minutes of tryouts and I was being outrun like I was standing still. My soccer skills were lackluster and without being at least among the fastest on the team, I was already done. And there was a guy so fast that as we came to the end of the first lap, he was a half a lap ahead of the lagging pack. Surely the other players could compensate for their lack of blazing speed with their scoring ability, their knowledge of the game, and their ability to control the ball. Now I had nothing. And as we finished the lap, the kid whose speed was unparalleled stood with the coach, waiting for our late arrival. And I nearly lost hope altogether, right from the start.

And there have been times in my life when I feel like I have been shot out of a cannon. The presence of God is pervading my very existence from day-to-day, and I am experiencing his love for me in dramatic ways. I wake up in the morning ready to worship God and love my neighbors. On those days, in those times, it never occurs to me to be afraid.

But over the years, I have learned something through these times. They are much fewer and further between than I would like to admit. Most days I wake up and I need to slap myself in the face with the gospel and a cup of coffee. Most days I start out in dire need of a battle just to spend a moment in the presence of God before the morning gets away from me. In those most trying of days, I find the work of faith is to fight off my seemingly inevitable inclination to drift off into a cycle of fear, self-doubt, and despair. The question that faces me more often than not is whether I will succumb to a fear induced paralysis, or listen to the voice of Jesus. Some days are more successful than others. Most days I feel so far behind in my spirituality that I am tempted to lose hope altogether, right from the start. But then, I am thankful that I am given the gift of more time, like I was in that first tryout day.

Because it only took a few minutes those many years ago for the mystery to be revealed. Nausea caught up with the guy I once thought was the fastest man alive. As the group of prospective teammates came together, a wave of exhaustion hit the man who was impossibly fleet of foot. He had, in his inexperience, neglected to see the bigger picture. The first lap, after all, was only a warm up for the next three hours in the setting August sun. I never thought

I would learn so much about life from a nauseated teammate in warm-ups, but that day we all witnessed the truth of the words, "the race is not for the swift of foot."[6]

And I have learned this lesson for myself time after time in my own life. Those times I have felt the best, worked the hardest, ran the fastest, and impressed everybody around me have amounted to the spiritual equivalent of nausea on an August afternoon. Life indeed is a marathon, and not a sprint.

And I wonder what life was like for Peter after that Pentecost. His life was clearly changed. He had taken a remarkable step from being dominated by his fear to becoming a courageous, self-sacrificing leader in the church. If history is correct, Peter's story ends with his own crucifixion, his cross turned upside down so that in following after Jesus, his story would be subservient to the man he believed to be God.[7] But we would not be doing Peter justice if we assumed he was suddenly cured of his insecurities. Peter was still trying to figure it out even to his dying day.

I think about his story of a vision Peter had of the heavens becoming a tablecloth before him with succulent, however unclean farm animals, ducks and even reptiles (frog-legs, anyone?). A voice told him: "Rise, Peter; kill and eat."[8] And we expect his answer of, "No!" Peter was a leader in the church. Jesus had handpicked him to lead this new way of life in the Spirit. He was not about to jeopardize his righteousness to obey any voice in a vision. And so the voice calls out to him a second time. The voice calls a third time. Finally, the voice of the Lord has had enough, and, almost as if he is stepping out of this rich, poetic scene, he says, "What God has made clean, do not call common."[9] Was it a sincere desire to keep the law of God that kept Peter from obedience, or was it his own fear of this new order of life?

We could give Peter a pass on the vision story, after all, it was a fairly big deal for him to change his eating habits, but his fellow

6. Ecc. 9.11.

7. Berry, *Foxe's Book of Martyrs*, 13.

8. Acts 10:13.

9. Acts 10:15.

Apostle Paul gives us a side of Peter that makes him look all too human. Makes him look too frail. In his letter to the Galatians, Paul tells the story of an altercation between the two of them. Peter, it seemed, was living out what he had learned in his aforementioned vision. He was eating and drinking with, and bringing the gospel to the Gentiles. And then some important, perhaps well-respected Jews came along and Peter repented of his repentance. Paul tells us, "When that conservative group came from Jerusalem, he cautiously pulled back and put as much distance as he could manage between himself and his non-Jewish friends."[10]

What? Peter, selling out his friends? No, not him! He had come so far! The coming of the Spirit changed his life! He walked in love, worked for global inclusion, and went out to seek the outsiders! Peter was finally getting the message he had heard and seen from Jesus. How could he take such a step back?

You know, I think I have a pretty good idea of how Peter felt. He must have felt like that kid on the soccer field, regretting the pace he had set for himself. He had been up for so long that he had put a bit of distance between his denial of Jesus and his story of becoming the Rock of the church. But it turns out he was still on his way to becoming complete in his love. It turns out that Peter and I have a lot in common.

But I bet his reaction was a bit different the second time he wimped out under pressure. After he denied Jesus three times, he weeps bitter tears, and I am sure he felt the same sadness as he ditched his friends, but I bet Peter had a better plan to deal with his cowardice this time.

This time, he could point back to the time when Jesus forgave him. Peter remembered that three times Jesus had asked him if he wanted the love he had to give. He remembered the three charges to: "feed (his) sheep."[11] And he remembered that, in spite of his first failure, God was not done with him. I bet he carried that experience into this second repentance.

---

10. Galatians 2:11. (The Message Translation)
11. Jn. 21:15–19.

Peter was learning the lesson that God's mission of chasing his fear with love was a process. And so am I.

The fear that I have known is not intended to stay around forever. One day, when Jesus' work in me is completed and I stand in his presence, I will love perfectly. I will not fear myself. I will not fear the world. My fear of God will be clean, pure, and look more like what we call: "reverence and awe" than what we call: "terror." On top of all of that, I will be transformed into a man who loves purely.

But along the way, from today until then, I know, like Peter, that forgiveness is mine. I know that he will use me, even though I fall into cowardice all too often. And most importantly, I know that I am loved. God is for me.

All of this I know because of what we Christians know as the gospel of Jesus.

6

A Love that Proves Itself

"(Jesus) has been manifested in a human body for this reason only, out of the love and goodness of his Father, for the salvation of (humankind)."[1]

Have you ever been hopelessly in love? I mean the type of love that reduces even the master wordsmith Bob Dylan to crumble into writing songs like "I Want You," ones that essentially loop the title for three and a half minutes?"[2] Have you ever been in so deep that you would do anything to win his or her affection? The things we do for love; well, at least the things we say for love.

Years ago, I fell in love, and since I was encountering Dylan for the first time, I knew it was for real. And she seemed to like me for whatever reason, especially at the beginning. We worked together, and even though we tried to keep our relationship professional during business hours, most times we would spend the entire shift making everybody in the place uncomfortable and, more than likely, annoyed. Life was good and times were easy and as the spring sprung that year, for the first time, I had somebody to profess my love to. And my words were pretty impressive at the time.

Sometimes I would even wow myself with my compliments, comparing her teeth to the modern-day equivalent of a flock of

1. St. Athanasisus, *On the Incarnation*, 26.
2. Dylan, *I Want You.*

sheep, and her hair to a less functional, though in every other way superior, version of Rapunzel's. I could not be clearer in my message of love to her. I was sure she had no doubt that I was crazy about her.

And like I said, I was just getting into Dylan, so I was not quite to *Blood on the Tracks*.

But I got there, soon enough. And I have to be honest; I was shocked by the news that she wanted to spend some time apart. So I took a quick inventory of everything a guy in his early twenties knew about love. Did I buy her flowers? Yes. Did I recite, and even write a little poetry? Yes. And it is a given that I am handsome devil, so it had to be something else. But what could be her problem? Who knows, I did everything I could to describe my love to her. Maybe she got tired of listening to Dylan.

I was heartbroken but I had said all there was to be said. And she had turned down my offer of love. How could she be so unaffected by my words of love? I had nothing to say. And what could I do? All I had to offer were words and she had stopped believing them. I had yet to learn that love is something that could not be described. And even less is it merely something to promise. It had to be shown. It had to be experienced. Love cannot be passive. Nor can it thrive in a world of words alone. It has to take on hazardous action.

Jesus loved to tell stories about love that took hazardous action. Just a couple of days before his arrest, he told a story about a landowner who goes on a journey, leaving his property to his managers.[3] When he sends a servant for rent they kick him out, roughing him up a bit before sending him on his way, empty-handed. There have been so many changes since the days of Jesus but some things are predictably similar. Renters are required to pay money on time, or else. Penalties are inevitable for whoever cannot come up with the rent on the first of the month. But this is a peculiar sort of landowner. He sends a second servant to collect the rent.

---

3. Matt. 21:33–46.

Things go no better for the second servant, who is promptly bludgeoned with rocks. So the landowner sends a third. They finish the job on him, murdering their landowner's messenger.

Can you imagine something so outrageous? The tenants have turned their rented land into a militia headquarters. The situation sounds more and more like a job for the SWAT team! What would you do if you were the landowner? If you were interested in preserving your wealth, your reputation, your property, your children's inheritance or even your self-respect, you would raise up an angry mob. Anybody would. Except for this landowner. But the landowner is persistent. He sends servant after servant, affording his tenants chance after chance to turn from their hateful, spiteful ways. But his message of patience and mercy goes unheard.

The landowner hatches a magnificent plan. He will send his son. "Surely," he thought, "they will respect my son!"[4] What a crazy, haphazard plan! If you were the landowner's friend, you would never let him do anything resembling this! And what if you were the son? "Hey Bobby, can you run down to the farm and ask those boys politely if they can pay their rent? Also, would you ask them if they would be willing to pick up a third or so of my servant's funeral bill?" I feel like I would do anything for my dad, but I would never, in a million years, consider running that errand for him. Then again, this seems to be a different kind of a son, too. He takes after his father. And so he goes–obediently–to the enemies of his father.

The inevitable conclusion to Jesus' story is the murder of the son. What else would happen to him? He is led, like a sheep into slaughter, out of obedience and love for his father. Then Jesus turns the question. "When therefore the owner . . . comes, what will he do to those tenants?" Here is another inevitability. He will put those wretches to a miserable death and let out the vineyard to other tenants who give him the fruits of their seasons."[5]

The landowner has given the original tenants years and years worth of opportunities to get serious. He has visited them time and again with a message of patience and an invitation for repentance

4. Matt. 21:37.
5. Matt. 21:41.

but he has been met with nothing but violence. Once he has given his son, though, things change. The message of repentance has turned into a statement of judgment. The message of love has turned into a sentence of wrath. But in the meantime, something strange has happened. The hatred of the original tenants has bought the entry for a new people. The murder of his son has turned into a ransom for a people who would have a new heart. The kind of heart that Ezekiel had spoken of so long ago.

Jesus' story seems to toss us and turn us around. Here we have a tale of patience that seems to have run out. Here we have justice and love in the same house. Here we have one people being judged with severity and another included in an unforeseen liberality. The love of God, it seems, has not run out, so much as the substance of that love has become starkly obvious. Everything stands and falls with the son.

This is why Jesus proceeded to talk about himself as a great foundational stone. Whoever is in opposition to the son will be crushed underneath his weight. Whoever makes a run at his authority by falling from above will break into pieces.[6] In the reckless mercy of the landowner, we see a glimpse of the heart of a God who will not be trifled with, even in his foolish mercy. Jesus not only highlights the long-suffering nature of his Father's love, he also calls attention to the timeliness of response to that love. Justice will either be done in the murder of the son or in the obliteration of the enemies who remain. Jesus' story functions as a warning to the hard-hearted and an invitation to the broken, and his life serves as the surest sign of not only the severity but much more the kindness of God.

And as I started to think about how the God of the universe chooses to get his love across, I started thinking about the girl again. I had always wondered why she got away, so years later I took her to a *Wilco* concert, which I figured was close enough to Dylan, and I let her know what I had always thought about her. Over the years, I found out that I wanted to try and see what it would mean to get my own love across.

6. Matt. 21:42.

On the way home, we talked about the old days, and it finally made sense when she told me the last thing I would have guessed. She had no idea that I even liked her, although I had once showered her with compliments My message had been lost in translation because my words stood alone. My love was not reckless. It was not active. My love was, to her, only words.

Then I received a rare opportunity to have second chance to communicate what I had felt for her all along. And this time, I started to learn how much harder it is to love somebody than it is to recite a poem. It seems so much more hazardous, so much more dangerous. It requires action. Love is better experienced than it is explained; practiced than professed.

The story of Christianity is of a God who is hazardously active in his love. He pursues. He discloses himself to us. He empties himself to get his message across to his beloved.

Can you believe that God loves you so passionately? Can you imagine that, in spite of everything he knows about your heart, your deepest desires, your darkest faults, your un-confessed secrets, your unfaithfulness to your spouse, your quick temper with your children and your constant complaints about work, money, emotional pain, and financial instability, he loves you enough to come here himself? God has become one of us for the express purpose of getting his love for us across. The thought is staggering.

That is why the love of God in the incarnation of Jesus is so impressive to me. God becomes fully and irreversibly immersed in humanity. He assumes all the risks and realities of love. He volunteers for the certainty of rejection. He willingly accepts the cost of loving an unlovable people. He commits to a non-committal, fearful people and is led, just like a lamb to the slaughter, for us.

For years and years he made his message clear through the prophets. Noah came and warned the people of the impending flood. God's messenger was mocked. Joseph came relaying the plan of God to his brothers. They beat him, left him for dead, saving his life only after running into bounty hunter to whom they sold him into slavery. Moses came proclaiming freedom for his people and found himself contending with the people of God for the next forty years of his life. The same happened to Isaiah, who was treated as a sideshow in a circus, Ezekiel, who was given a divine mandate to eat cow dung, and Jeremiah, who was in constant contention with a people he was commissioned with helping. One servant after another was sent to us and we treated every one of them like those wicked tenants in Jesus' story.

So the Father enacted a plan he had since before he created the world. He sent his son, like a lamb to slaughter. For us. Now his message of unfailing, passionate love has a definitive content. We know that he is for us because he sent his son. He has spoken to us with all the clarity at the disposal of the divine. In other words, he has acted in love. And His message is as simple as Dylan's. "I want you." The writer of the book of Hebrews said it like this:

"Long ago, at many times and in many ways, God spoke to our fathers by the prophets, but in these last days he has spoken to us by his Son . . ."[7]

7. Heb. 1:1–2.

7

Compelling Love

HAVE YOU EVER WONDERED why Jesus spent thirty-three years on earth before he died? I know I sure have.

And I know there are a million good reasons that justified Jesus' life. He had to explain what he was about to do on the cross and the world changing nature of his coming resurrection. He had to heal the sick. He had to raise the dead. He had to cleanse the lepers. He had to perform the fan favorite of changing the water into wine. Who else was going to stand up to the hypocritical Pharisees? Who else could feed the 5,000, and the 4,000?

Then you have your specific reasons for Jesus' life pertaining to his death. The law of God is blood for blood. Bulls and goats could never get the job done. God's mysterious, yet perfect justice demands human blood for human blood. If we look at it this way, Jesus had to become a card-carrying member of the human race because the bottomless pit of wrath we had incurred on ourselves could only be land filled by one with bottomless righteousness, and holiness. Somewhere in the distance we remember one of those verses from Hebrews, "without the shedding of blood there is no forgiveness of sin."[1] If Jesus had a different kind of blood than ours, well, we would be up the proverbial creek without the proverbial paddle.

---

1. Heb. 9:22.

So it makes sense that Jesus had to become a human, right? If there was ever going to be a payment for our sins, then there had to be a perfect human being to give his blood. Seeing as how we all fall miserably short of saving our brothers and sisters, let alone ourselves, God humbles himself to become human.

And while the death of Jesus does require the prior life of Jesus, we are missing out on everything if we stop here. So far all we have talked about is death, which, granted, is a worthy subject, and one that is key to the gospel story.

But what about life; does the gospel say anything about life, or is it just for death?

I remember my brother, Jay, and I talking years ago about a friend's sermon. Now, keep in mind that I was a theology major and Jay was a communications major. I was reading John Calvin for the first time, which is a dangerous endeavor. For you kids scoring at home, an 18-year-old reading the Reformers is sure to produce a level of arrogance that could make anybody blush. As I read the *Institutes of the Christian Religion*, I looked over at my brother (who, incidentally, was busy catching up on some baseball statistics and neglecting his soul!). It was getting lonely at the top of my spiritual perch, so I though I might stoop down and engage with the commoners, down there, busy thinking about something less than theology.

I started off with a simple question I knew we could agree on: "What did you think of Jarrett's sermon?" My best buddy had just ripped off a compelling exhortation from the book of Romans.

"It was alright, I guess," came his shocking reply.

My own brother: unmoved by sermonic perfection. I pressed him.

"What do you mean, alright?"

And, improbable as it must have been at the time, his answer actually made a pious theology student self momentarily humble. This is what he said: "The sermon was great. The only problem is that it was all about death. If somebody put a gun to my head right now I would have all the right answers, but what if I just go on living? How do I live?"

He had a point.

We find ourselves, all too often, unprepared for the most mundane and predicable miracle we encounter constantly: the miracle of more time. For every dramatic life and death scenario we find ourselves in there are millions of seemingly pointless moments. The true challenge lies in finding a way to live well.

But we know the dark, sultry downtowns of our hearts need a beautification if they will ever be a clean enough setting for the gospel plot to unfold.

The story of redemption is not only too beautiful for us to write, it is also far too simple to construct. Only a human can die for human. Only an innocent person's life is capable of redeeming the life of the guilty. This has the makings of a great story. The type of story we could never write.

One such story is Victor Hugo's *Les Miserables*. In this story, the good-hearted priest sacrifices his rights, wealth, security, and justice for the life of a despicable convict. The innocent pays his life for the guilty. Tragic? Heroic? Epic? Surprising? Frustrating? Good stories have a way of finding themselves retold. Great stories have a way of getting to our core.

And so the story that will lead us from the debilitating terror of one anther, our surroundings, and our failures to a well-grounded fear of God that places all fears in their proper perspective, to a life of freedom begins with a great story. And great stories are made of great characters that must face their fear. But there is another common element in these stories that move us: connection. Even if the innocent dies for the guilty, the fact remains that unless we have a personal connection, the best we can do is admire. We identify with even the greatest of characters before we can expect their lives to make a difference in the way we see the world.

I think about John Steinbeck's wandering outlaw, Tom Joad in *The Grapes of Wrath*. Joad, like many of Steinbeck's characters, is a walking contradiction. On one hand, when we meet him, he has given up on finding any higher purpose in life. He has been institutionalized, spending his last handful of years as an inmate for a brawl that ended in the death of his opponent. Though Joad has given up fully on all things spiritual, it is he who brings the struggling Reverend Jim Casy back into the faith. Though he is a murderer, and twice before the story ends, Joad's unquenchable thirst for justice, and equality, even as he doggedly provides for his family.

Joad leaves us with this: "Wherever they's a fight so hungry people can eat, I'll be there. Wherever there's a cop beatin' up a guy, I'll be there . . . I'll be in the way kids laugh when they're hungry an' they know supper's ready. An' when folks eat stuff they raise an' live in houses they build- why, I'll be there . . ."[2] These are more than admirable words; these are words with power because we identify with the man. We want what he wants.

Or think about Frodo Baggins in J.R.R. Tolkien's *The Lord of the Rings* stories. Here is a little hobbit that is in over his head. The world is a frightening place to Bilbo, yet he knows what to do. We love Frodo because we identify with him–in his need for community, in his desire to do what is right, in his desire to have the power of the ring for himself, in his conflict, his successes, and his failures. When he steps up and volunteers to take the responsibility of the ring, we cheer. When he wades through the marshlands, we tremble. When he sleeps next to Gollum, we are suspicious. In the end we are changed not simply because he is a great character, but because he is like us.

For all the reasons we may identify with a great character, a common theme is that they are plagued by fear. They are mysterious, vulnerable, and at times, you are sure that they are beyond their breaking point. The journey ahead seems too great, too difficult, too dangerous, and yet we need them to press on. Yet there is no story if they quit, if they give in. The commonality we feel is paired with a need for them to do what we feel we could never do. We need them to face their fears. We need to have a reason to believe that these characters could make it through. Great characters draw us into the story, out of our settled resignation. They call us out of phraseology and into their reality.

The invitation into the gospel story is calling us into the life of the main character, the God-man, Jesus. It is useless to admire and respect the protagonist of this particular story. He demands to be followed. He demands to be loved. He demands to be identified with.

2. John Steinbeck, *The Grapes of Wrath*. (New York: Penguin Books, 1999), 419.

God does not leave us alone to figure him out. He reveals himself to us. He is proactive in his love. He becomes one of us. Jesus is God's declaration of identity, of solidarity with us. The main character of the story does not call us to identify with him so much as he identifies with us. This is a divine love. This is a powerful love. This is a transforming love.

And so as we reflect on the incarnation of God, we recognize that this will require change. We cannot expect to meet God and remain the same. We will either hide from him in addiction, bitterness, apathy, and hopelessness; or we will be caught up into his life, into the drama of his incarnation.

On the other side of this change lies true freedom. To get there, however, we must become acquainted with real fear. We must become acquainted with true repentance. We must start out on the journey marked by unreflecting obedience to Christ himself. We must move from standing on the outside, from admiration to experience.

Why is Jesus so special? Why does he demand our time, our hearts and our lives? What sets Jesus apart from the rest of us? Is there something intrinsic about him that draws us, or are we clinging to an outdated fable? It all seems so unbelievable, right? Over the top, even. Do not be afraid. He will show himself in time. And if you are making up your mind, consider some wisdom from Puddleglum, the Marsh-wiggle.

In C.S. Lewis' *The Silver Chair*, Puddleglum is a poor subterranean swamp-man who, along with the rest of the remnant of Narnia, is trapped in the middle of the earth, deep underground and forced into the service of the Underground Queen. The work is so toilsome and the life so dark that the Queen has everybody convinced that there is nothing above ground. The old world of Narnia, ruled by the great lion Aslan, has only been a dream. There is nothing more to the world than hard work and service to the state. One day Puddleglum decides he has had enough. In the face of the Queen's fierce argument, he says:

One word. All you've been saying is quite right, I shouldn't wonder. I'm a chap who always liked to know the worst and then put the best face I can on it. So I won't deny any of what you said. But there's one thing more to be said, even so. Suppose we have only dreamed or made up, all those things–trees and grass and sun and moon and stars and Aslan himself. Suppose we have. Then all I can say is that, in that case, the made-up things seem a good deal more important than the real ones. Suppose this black pit of a kingdom of yours is the only world. Well, it strikes me as a pretty poor one.[3]

Puddleglum the Marsh-wiggle broke the spell of the underground because he was unwilling to accept the dark, dim view of the world presented to him. He knew that there was untapped beauty waiting for him on the other side of faith. It would mean abandoning his inherited view of reality and walking into the unknown, but he had courage. He was willing to step in and experience the fulfillment of his heart's longing, even if that meant the death of what had become his reality.

I find myself, every few days, in the same position Puddleglum was in. I find myself blinded to the colors of the December sky. I find myself deafened to the song of the robin in the springtime. I find myself in a place of spiritual apathy and I can hear the very clear and cogent advice of the Queen. "This is all there is. Make money, enjoy your family, work hard, and have a good time."

It seems like a daily occurrence for the life of Christ to drive through the fog of my heart and pierce light into my eyes; sharp, bold, and penetrating light. Jesus is a character who changes everything. Do you love Tom Joad for his dedication to the unfortunate? Jesus came to "seek and to save the lost,"[4] He came expressly for the sick, the outcast, the lonely, the forsaken and the poor. Does Frodo Baggins inspire you to be a more faithful, dedicated man or woman? Does his love for his friends call you into a different kind of life? Jesus laid down his life for his friends.[5] He promises to put

3. Lewis, *The Chronicles of Narnia*, 663.

4. Lk. 19:10.

5. Jn. 15:13.

in a good word with his Father on our accounts.[6] His love for us knows no bounds.

Let the story of Jesus pull you in. Let him re-create your world. Let him meet you in the midst of your fear. Let him convince you that in all of this, he is for you.

6. 1 Tim. 2:5.

8

A God Who Has Been There

BACK IN MY COLLEGE days, I played on the baseball team. But it may be more accurate to say that I was a member of the team, rather than a player. My role on the team could best be described as a full-time pinch runner.

They give pinch-running assignments to one of two types of players. The first kind of pinch runner, a speedy little guy, strikes fear into the heart of the catcher and distraction into the mind of the pitcher. The second type of pinch runner is the guy on the team who is too vigilant to get picked off and not quite up to par as a hitter or fielder. Truth be told, I fell into the latter category.

For some reason, I have the impulse to play a little Bruce Springsteen in the background when I tell people about my high school glory days. I could pitch, I could field, and I could hit just enough to get by. My senior year, I came a pitch away from throwing a no-hitter, played every inning in the field–flawlessly, I might add– and even hit a couple of home runs to boot. The summer before my freshman year in college, I was ready to go. I was full of confidence. Then something happened. My competition turned from kids distracted by getting their first car and going to the prom to grown men. And these were big guys. And they were much, much better than I was. Suddenly, I was out of my league. It wasn't long before I was fighting to hang on to my last shred of confidence. It got so that I couldn't even meet my own standards of success anymore.

My feeling of significance was shaken I was overmatched and under-prepared.

But after that first year, I was determined to right the ship the next year. But my next year turned out to be my last.

That year was a tale of two coaches. I was a sophomore and I could not wait until fall baseball came around and I could prove that my freshman year's ineptitude could be written off as an aberration. All summer long I lifted weights, ran up and down hills and had my brother hit me ground ball after ground ball. I felt ready to tackle the odds and crack the starting lineup on opening day. One start was all I needed to show I was a ballplayer, not just a pinch runner. But fall ball played out like a bad dream. And coach George seemed to take an unhealthy amount of pleasure in my failure.

George was the new assistant coach that year and apparently he had slept on the wrong side of the bed one too many times because one day I muffed a few grounders out of a thousand in practice and I became his mortal enemy.

"Hobbs!" He would yell as I struggled to find myself, "You're killing me!" Looking back, his unkindness must have been about his own deeper issues, but at the time, all I could hear was his criticism. Coach George began to openly root against me in front of the other guys. When the ball was hit my way he would beg me to fail. Thinking about the scene it is more than a little ridiculous, but my friend Pete tells the stories of Coach George cheering (or jeering) me on, "Kick it Hobbs! Throw it away!" Needless to say, Coach George was not the most popular new assistant coach on the block, and his time at our school was short-lived. Over Christmas break, he was ousted. When we came back to practice in January, we met Coach Bell.

Coach Bell had played in the minor leagues for years and years and he was a little guy, like me. Coach Bell was the type of coach who believed in every one of his players. He would talk about "going to battle" with us. He would give us advice on improving our footwork around the second base bag. He would teach us to visualize success with every swing of the bat. But he did more than provide us with moral support. He identified with us. Coach Bell, as clearly as anyone I've known, was for us.

He recognized that his job was of more significance than preparation for game time. He was in the business of preparing us for life. Sure, he would get frustrated. He was passionate and he loved the game and knew how to play it the right way. I can remember times when I booted a ground ball in practice and he shouted a few choice words in my direction, but his words had a different undertone. Coach Bell genuinely wanted each of us to succeed. His criticism was born out of the confidence that each of us could perform his part and help the team. He may never have realized his ultimate dream, to play in the big leagues, but he was happy with his role in life. He loved his wife and his son. Coach Bell would tell us that, no matter what happened, he could go home and his wife and baby boy would be happy to see him. He could rest at night knowing that the work he did was good and meaningful. And his coachly sermons to the team were always entertaining at bare minimum. Sometimes, if you can believe it, they were like water to a parched soul.

He could tell story after story about famous pitchers he faced, successes and failures on the diamond, as well as his life as the daddy of a toddler. He loved to tell us stories and he loved to encourage us.

His sermons reached a crescendo one particular day. We had lost a couple of tough games in a row and playoff time was upon us. This was no time to lose heart. No time to abandon hope. Coach Bell sat us down and started his quintessential homily.

"Will," he said referring to our slugging senior first-baseman, "you are the leader of this team. Everybody looks up to you. Everybody depends on you to drive in that run, to step up under pressure. That starts to wear on you. I know. I have been that guy everybody relies on. I have been there."

Then he turned to our struggling, however slick-fielding freshman third-baseman, "Matthew, this is all new to you. You have been used to being the guy everybody looks to, but you are overwhelmed right now. You know you have more to contribute but you don't know quite how to find it. Be patient. I have been there, too."

And so Coach Bell addressed the team, one by one, identifying with us. Then he got to me.

"Hobbs, you know you are better than you have played and you are itching for playing time. I know you have to fight for every at-bat. I know what it is like to have your role diminished on the team. You don't want to be a career pinch runner. You want to step up but you are losing confidence. You are afraid. Don't worry. I have been there, too. I have walked in your shoes. I have struggled. I have felt like giving up and I have seen the end coming. But don't worry. I see where you are and I have been there."

Now, my mom could have said the same thing to me and many times she did, but I needed to hear it from somebody who had been through the exact trials I was going through, and had made it to the other side. Coach Bell was that guy.

In walking through success and failure with us, Coach Bell was painting a picture of what the writer of Hebrews had in mind when she or he wrote, "Therefore, he had to be made like his brothers (and sisters) in every respect."[1] He had to walk in our shoes. He had to share in the joys of childhood, the awkwardness of being a teenager, the freedom of early adulthood, the pressures of a career and ordinary family life. He felt the disconnection of life outside the immediate presence of his Father. His peers insulted him and the elders disregarded him. He stared death in the face and believed even then. Whatever we have been through, Jesus has been there.

Back in the middle of the fifth century, the leaders of the church got together in a place called Chalcedon to loudly discuss, and eventually to agree on the wording of what we know as the "two natures of Christ." How can we say that Jesus has endured all he has as a human, while remaining fully God? Can Jesus' endurance of sin count for anything if he could play a trump card every time he was tempted?

Think about the stories of him being tempted by Satan on the mountain, at the beginning of John's Gospel. Does Jesus' obedience to the Father count for anything if he was incapable of sinning? His perfect obedience only counts if is capable of sin, like the rest of us, or else who cares if he sinned or not?

There was another question connected to the two natures of Jesus. For instance, was Jesus partially human at one time and partially God at others? Was he more human when he ate with sinners

1. Heb. 2:12.

and more God when he wept over Jerusalem? The resounding answer in Chalcedon is "no." Jesus is fully God and Jesus is fully human. Always.

The Godhood and the humanity of Jesus are true "without dividing them into two separate categories, without contrasting them according to area or function. The distinctiveness of each nature is not nullified by the union (of divinity and humanity)."[2] This is what Martin Luther meant when he said, "This man you look at and you say 'this is God.'"[3] Two natures. One God. And he is for us.

In his letter to the church at Rome, the Apostle Paul connected this spiritual truth to the nature of our salvation.[4] Paul pointed out that, since the beginning, when Adam, the first human, turned his back on God, we have all shared a common curse called sin. With sin come death, pain, hatred, insecurity, selfishness, and despair. But when Jesus stepped into the world to be one of us, there is a new order to our relationship with God. Where we used to be in Adam, turned on God and on ourselves, we can now stand in Christ, whose obedience, love, and righteousness is ours.

Because he has become one of us, his life stands for ours.

We all have Coach George in our lives, pulling us down, and discouraging us. Maybe you feel that God is like that. Do you hear him rooting against you? Does the perfection of Jesus scare you away? How could you ever live up to the reputation of an older brother who is perfect? These questions haunt us until we reach the inescapable conclusion that we cannot live up to his standard–nor do we have to. The point of his obedience is to provide perfect obedience for us. The object of him living as perfect human was not only to show us how to live (Although his life certainly does this for us) but so much more, his life is meant to stand for ours. He is made perfect to impart perfection to his brothers and sisters. His obedience provides the type of help that only someone who has been where we are today can possibly hope to offer us.

<hr/>

2. Lieth, *Creeds and Confessions*, 36.

3. Bonhoeffer, *Christ the Center*, 78.

4. Rom. 5:12–21.

The suffering, trials, heartaches, lonely nights, and trying days of Jesus are for our good. That is why the writer of Hebrews applies Jesus' perfect obedience to us. "For because he himself has suffered when tempted, he is able to help those who are being tempted."[5] Our story seems too good to be true. God himself has suffered, has endured temptation, has put himself through the gauntlet of navigating life in the fallen, chaotic mess of life and has come out the other side. But it only gets better.

Coach Bell's words are only an echo of our story of the word become flesh. The Spirit speaks to us through Jesus' humanity and simply says, "I have been there."

What are you afraid of? Is death knocking on your door? He has been there. Where are your friends when you need them? He has been there. How can you believe the story when everything in my life seems to rise up against you? He has been there. Have you been neglected? He has been there. Have you been abused? He has been there. Humiliated? He has been there. Forgotten? He has been there.

This is not simply a connection that Christ has made with us. It is a promise that God is now inextricably bound together with us. Bonhoeffer wrote simply: "in the incarnation of Christ, the assurance is given that Christ is willing to take form amongst us here today."[6] That he has been where we have been is a promise that he will be where we are always.

He is the most compelling of characters. His story pulls us in. He meets us right in the midst of our fears, of our doubts, of our longings, of our broken hearts, of our last chances, and of our unbelief. He knows what we are up against. He knows from the ground level. But unlike us, he knows what it means to win. And he calls us into life inside of his victory right where we are, in the midst of meetings, funerals, marriages, careers, families, life, and death.

---

5. Heb. 2:18.
6. Bonhoeffer, *Ethics*, 88.

9

The Fulfilled Law

"Oh how I love your law. It is my meditation all the day."[1]

I read these words last week as my wife and I sat down over a cup of coffee. And to be honest, when I said them out loud, they sounded a bit foreign. I have been racking my brain since then, trying to remember the last time I spent a day just daydreaming about the law of God. There seem to be so many other things out there for me to meditate over: my successes, my failures, my hopes, and my fears. These are more the subjects of my thoughts from day to day.

And even though I have spent a good portion of my life studying the law of God, in church, in school, in seminary, I don't seem to be cured yet of my tendency to ignore Leviticus. And who would want to read an Old Testament, if we have a new one? That is a giveaway right there, if ever there was one! The Old Testament seems so pointless, so obsolete. If we want to be spiritual, we have to read the New Testament. If we want to be bored to tears, we read the Old Testament, complete with its dietary laws, Hittites, and Jebusites. And if that were not enough, what about the genealogies? Who can make sense out of the endless lists, let alone put their delight in them?

And then there is Jesus, coming and setting himself against the old ways, right? Was it not Jesus who said, "You do not put new

1. Ps. 119:97.

wine in old wineskins?"[2] Was it not Jesus who broke the Sabbath, stripping the weekly custom of its religiosity?[3] And was it not Jesus who came to make all things new?[4] Was it not Jesus who came to nullify the old law, nailing it, and our sins to his body on the cross?[5] And was it not Jesus who came to set all things right that had gone wrong with God and his people over the years?

Hasn't the object of our contemplation changed with the coming of Jesus, after all? The people of God way back then may have only had the Law as God's word to them, but we have more. And if we pay attention to Jesus, it seems that God's ways have changed and we have better things to dwell on, right?

Think of all the reasons we would have to think about without that pesky old Law, anyway! We could rejoice that God loves us enough to become human for us. We could rejoice that Jesus did what we could never do, in satisfying the demands of the law for us. We could rejoice that he died for us, taking on the last shot that the law had to offer him. Then we could rejoice that we did not have to do anything from here on out; just ride out this "forgiveness" thing for as much as it's worth.

But Jesus never had a problem with the law. In fact, he alone could meditate on the revelation of God to humanity without reservation. He would not have to read quickly over the commandment where he learned not to steal. He was no thief, why would he hate the law? And he would not be threatened by the prohibition of murder. Forgiveness, not hate, was the consistent posture Jesus had toward his enemies. Neither would he be intimidated by the commandment not to commit adultery, nor the one not to covet the things his neighbor owned. He was content.

It is we who have the problem, not the law.

This is what Paul said in his letter to the Romans, when he was lamenting his inability to please God.[6] He refers to the law as

2. Mk. 2:22.

3. Mk. 2:24.

4. Rev. 21:5.

5. Col. 2:14.

6. Rom. 7:7–25.

both, "good," and "spiritual." But he calls himself "sold under sin." We identify with him when he says, "nothing good dwells in me, that is my flesh." Paul is a mess, just like us. But he tells us that he is the problem, not the law.

I consider myself a pretty good driver, regardless of what those around me say. And I have some statistics to back that up. In over ten years of driving, I have had one ticket, the merits of which I will contest to my dying day. You might understand, then, why I was shocked–outraged, even–that in my first February living in the state of Washington, when I received a hat trick of speeding tickets. By my count, that would be over 140 months on the road with a clean record (I cannot, in good conscience, count the contested ticket against my score, but that's another story for another time!), and three tickets in thirty days. One of those sticks out to me, in particular.

I was running late for work and had just called my boss to confess my lack of time management skills. His response did not set my heart at ease. "Well, just get here as soon as you can." Then, click. Maybe I am alone in this, but sometimes all of the stress in my body centralizes at the bottom of my right foot. I was determined to make up time (and I was) until I saw the flashing lights in the rear view. I must say, that the policeman who pulled me over was about the nicest guy I have ever encountered wearing a baton and wielding pepper spray, but there was no doubt as to the outcome. As much as I would have liked to deny it, this one was completely my fault.

And as he wrote the ticket, I sat in my truck and thought about the law. You know, it was not the fault of my boss that I was late. It was not the fault of the state that the speed limit was there. It was not the fault of the policeman, who was only doing his job to keep the streets clean, and safe from law-breakers. I had nobody to blame but myself.

And a strange thing happened. I saw that morning that justice is a good thing. How could any business run with its employees coming in anytime they felt like it? And how could a city be safe without laws to prevent people from making up time by endangering lives, however skillful the driver may be? And how could the policeman look himself in the mirror if he shirked the doing of justice that he had sworn to carry out? The law was right, I was wrong. And I gained an appreciation for the law that only cost me a couple of hundred dollars.

I think the same thing is happening for Paul as he writes about his failure to keep the law of God. He is not asking the Lord to take away the nasty constraints of those Ten Commandments, but to give him strength, desire, and commitment to obey them with a thankful heart. He is not asking for the nullification of the law, but for a heart of flesh that can be affected by it. He confesses his need to be made new.

And I think this is more to the point of the view of the God-man, when it comes to the law. This is why he told the disciples, right from the start, "Do not think that I have come to abolish the law and the prophets, I have not come to abolish them, but to fulfill them."[7] In fact, Jesus warns us against even getting a comma out of place as we look back at the law of Moses. It needs to matter to us that it was Shamgar, not Ehud, who was the son of Anath, and killed 600 Philistines with an ox goad.[8] We have to deal with the fact that the law commands us to rest on the Sabbath. And we have to deal with the fact that we are incapable of living up to any and all of the demands of the law.

But for those of us who have become accustomed to facing our incompetence, it is not enough to throw up the white flag on obeying Christ. It is not enough to start off with the conclusion of Luther, to sin boldly. We begin with obedience. In the words of Bonhoeffer, "only those who believe obey and only those who obey believe."[9] Belief and obedience are not as remote as we would make them out to be.

We begin by committing ourselves the law of God. We begin by sitting under the revelation of God and allowing ourselves to be exposed for the law-breakers that we are. Only then will we be able to appreciate the fact that Christ has fulfilled the law for us.

7. Matt. 5:17.
8. Jud. 3:31.
9. Bonhoeffer, *The Cost of Discipleship*, 70.

In the life of Jesus, we see him constantly committed to fulfilling the law in every sense. He is the one who loves himself with all his heart, soul, mind, and strength. He is the one who loves his neighbor as himself. He is the one who puts his glory above all else, putting no idols before his Father. He is the one who takes the name of the Lord with the utmost sincerity. He is the one who not only keeps the Sabbath perfectly, even more, he corrected the slavish enforcement of minutia with a call back to rest. Then he becomes the eternal rest for his people.

He is the one who honors his parents. He is the one who upholds human life, saving us from our own self-murder. He is the one who keeps covenant. He is the one who gives us life abundantly, a life that had been stolen by the devil. He is the one who keeps his word. He is the one who is fully contented, happy, and joyful in his own nature. Jesus kept the law perfectly, wholly, and once for all.

In Jesus, we see a law that is holy, good, and fulfilled.

And the message of the gospel is that this law is now ours. We do not inherit a law that oppresses us, neither do we inherit a law that is nullified. We inherit a law that is fulfilled. We inherit, in our justification, a law that calls us new. We inherit, in our sanctification, a heart that loves, cherishes, and seeks to uphold this law, for no other reason than love for God, and love for neighbor.

Since Jesus fulfilled the law, it has become a gift to us. It not only points us toward our constant need for the righteousness that he gives us, but we find in it the substance of what it means to love.

What would our lives be like if we knew that, in Christ, even the law of God was for us?

10

The Suffering of the Divine

COMEDY? OR TRAGEDY?

That is the question that lies before *Stranger Than Fiction's*[1] protagonist Harold Crick. Harold is an IRS agent whose attention to detail is only matched by his fear of truly living his life. Because Harold fears pain, rejection, chaos, and most of all, death, he creates an absurdly regimented routine of isolation. Harold is the classic example of a man so paralyzed by the fear of death that he cannot live his own life. Instead of risking himself to love his neighbor, he falls back upon the letter of his own law.

Harold's life is turned upside down when, out of nowhere, he hears the voice of a woman narrating his life. It turns out this was the voice of his own novelist Karen Eiffel. She is writing a story in which Harold is the protagonist. As you may well imagine, the voice-over narration is unsettling and threatening to the safe little life Harold has constructed around him.

Harold begins to see his life as a story, although that original question haunts him day and night. Will his life have a happy ending and thus become a comedy? Or will his life end in tragedy? At first flustered, then disturbed, Harold's fear turns to terror when he finally comes to terms with his own life as a tragedy. He accepts life on the terms that he will, indeed, one day die.

1. *Stanger Than Fiction.*

Here is when the story gets good.

When Harold embraces the reality that he will one day die, he begins to truly live. He takes a few days off work, buys a Stratocaster, and moves in with his coworker. Harold also pursues a relationship with a beautiful, tempestuous baker. He has finally overcome so many of the fears that have kept him from living all these years and we rejoice at seeing his growth as a human being.

But then he finds out one more troubling fact about his writer. She has a habit of killing her main characters. Harold's old terror has now become desperation and determination to have a personal meeting with his author. Surely his life could not end in death if he could just meet with her.

Here is when the story gets really good.

When Harold and his author finally meet, she has already written the end of his story. His own death is now surely imminent. Through a series of events, Harold sits down to read his own story. The ending is brilliant. The ending is too poetic, too perfect, too full of life and love to avoid. The story must end with Harold's death. There is no other way.

Harold is a lot like us. Too afraid to live his life for fear of death, failure, tragedy and the like, he shuts out the world around him. That is, of course, until he understands that life is designed to lived well. It is not to be stored away and protected. He faces the fact that only his writer will choose the meaning of his life. And now he knows the end.

In a way, Harold's story is reminiscent of Jesus'. Jesus knew exactly the painful suffering that would soon come over him. Jesus knew that his best friends would soon jump ship. He knew that the cross was only hours before him. He knew his Father would look away from him, abandoning him on the cross. He knew he would die.

But he went willingly.

Jesus knew that his Father was writing a story too perfect for him to run away from his death.

Here is when our own story connects with his.

Jesus' story has now become our story. His trust has become our trust. His obedience has become our obedience. His death has become our death. What we had coming to us through a lifetime of sworn opposition to the rule of the divine, God himself sets right by taking our justice upon himself.

The cross of Jesus cancels our debt in the court of God. In going willingly to the cross, Jesus takes on the mess we have made of life. He takes away our fear of coming to God empty-handed and guilty. The death of Jesus is God's "no" to our own death. As Bonhoeffer wrote, "he bears the whole burden of mankind's separation from God, and in the very act of drinking the cup (of death) he causes it to pass over him."[2]

It was Thursday night in the Garden of Gethsemane when we see Jesus overwhelmed by fear. You know this place, right? His voice must have been cracking and halting as he spoke to his Father. "If you are willing, remove this cup from me."[3]

Jesus knew what was coming. He was about to be arrested and tried by the same people he came to liberate. It seemed his message of love and peace had struck a foul chord with his audience. The life that the Good Shepherd offered fell on deaf ears. The way of healing that the Great Physician offered was too controversial. Jesus saw the physical pain coming. He saw the insults from his people. He saw the pathetic fear of his friends in the face of trouble. He knew the wounds were coming. He knew the crown that awaited him the next day would be made of thorns, and his throne a wooden post.

For all the physical, psychological and emotional pain Jesus was going to experience, though, nothing was worse than the real suffering that awaited him.

In the Garden, Jesus was only hours away from being separated with his Father. A fracture was coming in the divine relationship. Jesus would cry out, in only a matter of hours, "My God, my God, why have you forsaken me?"[4] Jesus was stepping into utter abandonment for us. The time was upon him.

Back in the movie, everything changes as Harold finally comes to the conclusion that the author's ending for him was good. He would jump in front of a bus to save the life of a child. His life would

2. Bonhoeffer, *The Cost of Discipleship*, 92.

3. Lk. 22:42.

4. Matt. 27:46.

have a tragic end, but his end would mean a lifetime of beginnings for another. The ending is simply too poetic, too beautiful, too full of sacrifice, and too compelling to change.

And while it is subtle, there is a glimpse of joy in his eyes as he lives out the last moments of his life, mixed with the uncertainty of his coming death. It was the joy that lay in front of him that convinced Jesus to carry on, to step into his own death. He knew that his Father's plan was good.

That Jesus chose death on our accounts is not just good news. It is news that reorients reality. It changes everything. In the book of Romans, Paul wrote: "What then shall we say to these things? If God is for us, who can be against us? He who did not spare his own Son but gave him up for us all, will he not also with him graciously give us all things? . . . What shall separate us from the love of Christ? Shall tribulation, or distress, or persecution, or famine or nakedness, or danger or sword?"[5]

The message of Jesus is not that sufferings will not come. They will definitely come, if they haven't already. We will all bear our own cross and share in his sufferings. In the very next verse, Paul compares us like sheep to be slaughtered. Pain in all the ways it meets us, is sure to come. Loved ones will die suddenly. Friends will betray us. Health will leave us. Financial security may not come back once lost. Hard times have come and they will keep on coming at us. The message of Jesus is not that hard times are over but that there is one who stands with us in those times.

This past year, one of my best friends was diagnosed with cancer. Stunned, listening to the news, I tried to regroup and ready myself for an opportunity to provide words of comfort. After he was gracious enough to hear my stumbling, faltering words of hope, he began to show me what it is like to believe the promises of Christ while fighting for his life. And he hasn't stopped.

Another close friend has had a close family member killed in the line of duty. His faith too is a witness that God is for him. Even in the midst of grieving, he is able to bear witness to the peace of Christ.

---

5. Rom. 8:31–35.

They can have this hope because they have known the God who has given his son for them. In their suffering, they have not been alone. There is one who suffers with them. They are able to face their own fears because Jesus faced his own fear in the garden. And he stepped willingly into his own death.

The cross is the most difficult part of our story. How can the Father love the Son and be willing to put him to death? How does hatred of sin and compassion come together? We don't have a category for the cross.

But because of the cross, we can be absolutely sure that God is for us.

Oh, and Harold? He stepped willingly into his own death. But as his author watched her drama unfold, she realized that there had to be more. The story simply couldn't end with Harold being dead. So she writes him a resurrection.

When she does, she is questioned, "Why not leave the story at its natural conclusion? why muddle it up with a twist that seems too good to be true?" Her answer tells us why this story goes on. "If a man does know he's about to die and dies anyway. Dies willingly, knowing he could stop it then–I mean, isn't that the type of man who you want to keep alive?"

Death is never allowed to have the final word.

11

Love that Reaches to the Depths

ONCE I WAS A part of a small country Baptist church whose pastor had decided to start a practice of the congregation confessing the faith together and he chose the Apostles' Creed as a starting place. The first Sunday you could feel the tension in the room as he introduced the idea of standing up (just like the Presbyterians!) and agreeing together about the nature of God, and of our faith. It seemed like everybody was ok at the beginning. "I believe in God, the Father Almighty, Maker of heaven and earth, and in Jesus Christ, his only son, our Lord." Nobody knew quite what to make of this seemingly archaic practice, but we were all playing along. Until the next phrase: "who was conceived by the Holy Ghost, born of the Virgin Mary."

Now, maybe it is because Mary is so venerated by the Roman Catholic church that so many of us are afraid to give her a place in history, especially one so close to the center of our faith. Or maybe it is just because she was a woman. Either way, the silence when we reached the fourth clause of the Creed was so palpable you felt like you could reach out and touch it.

It was took a couple of weeks for everybody to get on board with the whole Mary ting. After all, the fact that Jesus was Mary's son seems to be a pretty important piece of the puzzle.

The next battle our pastor had to fight was over a phrase that some church leaders today still contend should not be a part of the old Creed. And it's hard to blame them. It is a phrase that is wrapped in mystery.

"He descended into hell."

When I first heard these words, I was stunned. Could Jesus go to hell? Is that a possibility?

The early church certainly thought it was more than a possibility. While this may be a forgotten belief in today's church, historians say that the belief itself is found in writing as far back as the second century, just seventy years after the death of Jesus.[1]

Biblical writers like Paul, John, and Luke seem to have glossed over the work Jesus did in the three days between his death and resurrection, but the belief is not left out of the record entirely. Peter thought it was important enough to point out to a people on the run.

Peter, in his first letter to the exiles, pointed back to this time when he wrote, "For Christ also suffered once for sins, the righteous for the unrighteous, that he might bring us to God, being put to death in the flesh but made alive in the spirit, in which he went and proclaimed to the spirits in prison, because they formerly did not obey."[2]

Was Jesus preaching to the dead in hell from Friday night till early Sunday morning? And what could possibly be the message those three days?

But the larger question is, "if Jesus descended into hell, what did he descend into?" Was it a fiery abyss akin to Daniel's lion's den? Did Jesus go to Dante's inferno and suffer white-hot torture at the hands of Satan? Or is hell more like a holding-place for the dead, like the dilapidated inter-world office of the dead depicted in Tim Burton's *Beetlejuice*? Or is hell more like that place we fall into when the hand of God drops us, like the spider into his burning wrath that Jonathan Edwards used to preach about so many years ago? Each of these versions of hell carries with them their own difficulties, particularly when we imagine Jesus descending into them.

1. Leith, *Creeds and Confessions*, 22.
2. 1 Pet. 3:18–20.

How much authority does Satan possess authority in hell? Does he have enough authority in hell to torture Jesus? This is the picture that C.S. Lewis painted in his classic *Narnia* stories. Aslan, the great lion is tied down to the stone table to be sacrificed to buy the freedom of all Narnians and the forgiveness of the impulsive Edmund. And who receives the sacrifice? Who is squealing with glee but the White Witch? She tears his mane, she whips his back; it is not holy justice that is satisfied but the bloodthirstiness of the White Witch. Is this what happened to Jesus?

A host of other questions then arise from the untended ground. Is there an intermediary time in-between the time of now and eternity? These are not thoughts that are easy to take to bed and rest with. They haunt us because is forces us to deal with the weight of our sin.

We are brought face to face with the reality that our crimes against the eternal God have incurred an eternal judgment. We deserve hell. But what are we talking about when we say that?

What seems clear about heaven is that we are in; and what seems clear about hell is we are out. Heaven is the fullness of God's presence and pleasure; hell is the active absence of God's goodness. Hell is the place of banishment, exclusion, wandering, and isolation.

Does that sound like a light sentence, to be actively excluded from the presence of God? Is hell incomplete without fire, brimstone, and a ruling devil? Is it a small thing to be forever cut off from God? What if we were to say that the entire good of heaven is the presence of God and the entire ruin of hell is his absence?

To be clear, we have no idea what this absence is, really. In that place you would be hard-pressed to even pray with David: "If I ascend into heaven, you are there! If I make my bed in Sheol, you are there!"[3] We know a world where everything moves and dances to the rhythm of God's presence. Even on the darkest day in the most godless and evil place, God is with us. The troubling reality, however, is that there is a coming finality to our world and Jesus says that at the end of it all, some will be in and some will be out.

---

3. Ps. 139:8.

Jesus uses the word we translate as "outer darkness" in Matthew's gospel account three times. Once in the story of Jesus' healing of a Gentile soldier's son, when he told his disciples that one day the "sons of the kingdom"- that is, the Israelites who ignored and rejected his coming- will be thrown out and the believing Gentiles will be brought into the presence of God in their place.[4] Jesus speaks another time of a prince's wedding fest when nobody showed up. The servants went into the highways and hedges and compelled the homeless to dine and celebrate with the king. One guest apparently did not get the memo that it would be a good idea to dress up to this affair (imagine a guest who dishonors the host of a party he wasn't even originally invited to!), and he is cast out into this same "outer darkness."[5] Then the third time, Jesus told a story about the coming day when the Father will separate the sheep from the goats. It is time to draw the line between the headstrong and the obedient. Sheep are too simple to have their own agenda. Goats, on the other hand, are a conniving, scheming and willful kind. The sheep, he brings in and the goats are cast out into this same "outer darkness."[6] Final judgment gets no more final than that.

So now picture Jesus enduring that separation for us. He descends into hell. He goes to the place of full and complete abandonment from his Father. He is cut off. God actively abandoned his own Son, Jesus for us. He descended into hell for us. Jesus, as the writer of Hebrews wrote, "suffered outside the camp"[7] for us.

The reality of hell is no less hellish than this. Does this mean that hell is not as bad as it is cracked up to be? Far from it! This version is as bad as it can get. Think of your own deepest, darkest place. Can you imagine going through that time without the help of God, even if you hadn't seen his hand in that moment?

We cannot know the horrors of hell, let alone expect to comprehend the plunge of God into Godlessness that we confess. We

---

4. Matt. 8:12.

5. Matt. 22:13.

6. Matt. 25:30.

7. Heb. 13:12

cannot fathom the depths of suffering that Jesus took on for us but we can be deeply thankful that we have this little phrase to pore over: Jesus descended into hell.

Because he descended we need never know the horrors of hell. Because he descended we need never know what it means to be "out," in the true sense of the word. Because he descended, we need never know what it means to wander alone. Because Jesus descended into hell we can bank on the presence of God now and always.

Think about how this changes the difficulties we face every day. Work, family, life, death, betrayal, divorce, marriage, children, hunger, pride, and addiction: none of these things can cut us off from God. In fact, what we learn through hard times is that God is nearer than ever.

Consider Bonhoeffer's words: "Suffering means being cut off from God. Therefore those who live in communion with him cannot really suffer . . . He bears the whole burden of humanity's separation from God, and in the act of drinking the cup he causes it to pass over him . . . Hence while it is still true that suffering means being cut off from God, yet within the fellowship of Christ's suffering, suffering is overcome by suffering, and becomes the way to communion with God."[8]

Here is a man who spent the last several years inside German prisons and was hanged to death because of his belief in and witness to the person of Jesus. He was in communion with God and yet he suffered a whole lot more than I ever have. Here is a guy who was executed by the Nazis telling us that suffering, in the sense of being cut off from God, is not for Jesus' friends. Suffering instead is what marks us out as his. Suffering draws us into the love of God. This can only be true if Christ has suffered wholly for us. It can only be true if Jesus has been once cut off from God, and in his being cut off, we are–paradoxically–drawn in permanently.

We could dismiss a stuffy theologian who makes such a bold claim. We may even overlook a well-meaning friend when we are offered promises that seem so empty. But when a man who suffered to the end can say something like this, we normally stand up and take notice.

8. Bonhoeffer, *The Cost of Discipleship*, 92.

In the cross of Jesus, he has taken on our suffering, the exclusion that we have deserved, and returned to give us a share in the life of God.

And because Jesus descended into the depths of separation, we need never fear hell itself. Because he suffered outside the gate, we need never know what it means to be "out." Because he went willingly to the place of abandonment, we need never know what it means to wander alone. Because Jesus descended into hell, we can bank on the presence of God now and always.

The Son of God descends to God-less-ness for his enemies, and in doing so, he makes his enemies his friends, his brothers, and his bride. This is the fatal blow to death itself: that Jesus is not afraid (nor ashamed!) to go to hell itself to buy us back to himself. We rejoice with Martin Luther: "For us, through Christ, hell has been torn to pieces and the devil's kingdom and power utterly destroyed, for which purpose he died, was buried, and descended, so that it should no longer harm or overwhelm us."[9]

He descended into the depths of hell to rescue us from what we had coming. What do we have to fear?

He is for us.

---

9. Luther, *Historical Introductions to the Book of Concord*, 193.

12

The Difference Between Jesus and Obi-Wan Kenobi

"Jesus rose again as a man, and by so doing he gave men the gift of the resurrection."[1]

Have you ever noticed that, when Mary, Peter and John show up at the tomb of Jesus, his grave clothes are still there?[2] When John re-told the story, he remembered that the linens used to wrap his face were laying a few steps from the cloths used to wrap his body. Sometimes pictures stay with you, the image of his master's empty tomb must have replayed in his mind a million times before he wrote down the story. Why include that little detail, though?

Apparently John loved to include seemingly meaningless detail in his version of Jesus' life and times on earth. It was from John that we heard about the best fishing expedition recorded in biblical times. The disciples caught 153 fish in one cast. But why not say that the disciples caught a ton of fish? And what an odd number! Not forty, like the years in the wilderness. Not twelve like the number of tribes in Israel, and the number of disciples. Not even twenty-three, as a hidden, mysterious prophesy of Michael Jordan's future reign over the nets of his day. Nope. 153.

---

1. Bonhoeffer, *Ethics*, 132.
2. Jn. 20:5.

John wants us to know that his stories are for real. There really was a catch of a ridiculous amount of fish because there really was a physically resurrected Jesus commanding the real ocean to produce said bass, salmon, or whatever comes out of the Sea of Tiberias. After they caught and apparently catalogued the fish, they had breakfast together–a real breakfast–the once-dead Jesus and his disciples. This is earthy. This is real. This has to do with the day-to-day stuff of life. Why was there 153? Because that is how many fish they caught. John was there. He was an eyewitness, and he must have counted at least a large pile of them! John wants us to know that Jesus is all about the stuff of life.

From the first words of John's gospel story we hear this message. The word has become flesh and has taken up residence among his people.[3] God has entered into the details of reality and lived with us. What a great way to wrap up the story, this word of God invading the very minutia of life. Jesus meets us in reality. Messy and odd as it can be. And this will be the new order of things. This is the new type of life that Jesus gives us through conquering death.

Growing up, it did not matter how many times I heard about the resurrection. All I could picture was Obi-Wan Kenobi. If you are too cool to have seen the *Star Wars* movies a million times, I will allow you temporary access into the world of the nerds.

Obi-Wan Kenobi is an old man when we meet him at first (In the original non-prequel editions, at least). Luke Skywalker, a twenty-something dude who lives in the desert with his aunt and uncle, buys a droid (because that was what sand-ranchers a long time ago, in a galaxy far, far away spent their time doing) who bears a secret message. It appears a beautiful princess is looking for some crazy old hermit who lives on top of a mountain, named "Ben." Ben, of course, is the nickname for the strange old rebel fighter, Obi-Wan Kenobi.

Long story short, Luke finds, and ends up being mentored by Obi-Wan, flying on the Millennium Falcon, and saving the galaxy. Also, Luke finds he has a mysterious connection to the evil (and frankly awesome!) helmet-clad Sith Lord who went by the handle of "Darth Vader."

---

3. Jn. 1:14.

The story takes a turn in a battle with Vader when Kenobi suddenly has an epiphany. If he keeps fighting, he would be able to assist Luke in the seemingly impossible task of balancing the force, but he would be limited in his powers by time and space, along with his aging body. He was an old man and he could only be in one place at one time. If he were to die, however, he could be the voice of encouragement and moral support that Luke could use down the road, to do battle with the dark side of the force. And so Obi-Wan Kenobi lowers his light-saber and submits to death.

Now, I cannot be sure about Obi-Wan Kenobi's knowledge of the afterlife, so I will stop short of saying his plan was dumb. He may have just been confused, after all.

The problem with Ben Kenobi's so-called resurrection is that it was not for real. He only came back as a ghost. Maybe everybody was so busy with constructing the Death Star that they had not thought to invent cell phones or email, because anybody's grandma can be a source of moral support, especially if they have the help of Internet cafes and wifi. And when Obi-Wan Kenobi came back from the dead, he came back as an ethereal mirage that could only be seen outside of an Ewok campfire.

Is this all we mean when we say that Jesus "rose again?" Are we saying that now Jesus' jurisdiction is limited to some realm beyond? Are we saying that he lives, but only in the sense that he is there to offer us moral support when we are down in the dumps?

Is the resurrected God-man disinterested in our day-to-day lives? If Jesus has conquered death, how can he concern himself with little problems like a sick child, an annoying coworker, a harsh boss, or a demeaning boyfriend?

I mean, where was Obi-Wan Kenobi when Luke was falling in love with Princess Leia, his long-lost sister? Couldn't he have appeared to him there? Or did he have more important things to worry about? He would provide direction to Luke in all matters Force, but in none of the small things! And when you compare everything to the destiny of the galaxy, I suppose even falling in love with your sister seems irrelevant.

In the same way, the salvation and history of mankind dwarfs any problems we encounter on a regular basis. Are we left to ourselves in these times, while Jesus gets ready for his next public appearance?

It becomes quickly apparent that a spiritually resurrected Jesus is not enough. We need him to be flesh and blood.

Because what real power did the ghost-leader provide to Luke? What true interest could he possibly take in his life? He was only interested in the cause. He only provided help to Luke that would directly benefit the cause of bringing balance to the force. Luke's welfare, to Obi-Wan Kenobi, quickly becomes a means to an end. And if Jesus did not rise again as fully human–as true flesh and blood human–we would be in a similar predicament.

Paul reflected on this same possibility, that the resurrection was only real in philosophical sense. To him, everything seemed to stand and fall here. He wrote: "If Christ has not been raised, then our preaching is in vain." It gets worse. "If Christ has not been raised, your faith is futile and you are still in your sins." And worse. "If in Christ we have hope in this life only, we are of all people most to be pitied."[4]

All of our lives stand and fall at this one point. If Jesus did not rise to new life as every bit human as he was when he walked among us, then there is no coming resurrection for us. And if that is true, then we are living intentional, purposeful lives only until we run out of days. You may think it is still worth doing good for goodness' sake, but not me. And certainly not Paul! If Jesus rose from the dead like Obi-Wan Kenobi rose from the dead, as a ghost meant for moral support, then we are wasting valuable days living quiet, sober, and loving lives.

And what about church? You may be so in love with the idea of loving your neighbor that you can love without having been loved by God, but as for me, I am out. The last thing I would choose to do is to wake up early on Sunday, miss a ton of football games, sing songs about a dead guy, and listen to somebody prattle on about how to live life. As if church would have any relevance to life at that point!

Paul tells us that if Jesus is still dead, we may as well live it up because being good for goodness' sake is a waste of time. But he is not dead. That is the critical point. "In fact Christ has been raised

4. 1 Cor. 15:12–19.

from the dead, the first fruits of those who have fallen asleep."[5] Now, each and every moment, every detail, has become spiritual, vital, purposeful, and alive. The resurrection of Jesus as true human is more like J.R.R. Tolkien's imagined world in *The Lord of the Rings* than the creation of George Lucas.

In a similar scene to Obi-Wan Kenobi's battle with Vader, Gandalf the Grey wizard squares off against the evil, giant Balrog on the bridge of Khazad-Dum. The company of the Ring, which includes a couple of hobbits, a dwarf, an elf, and two men, have run into an army of orcs (Which is bound to happen if you take the Ring to Mount Doom). Gandalf the Grey wizard steps forward, and defends his friends, even though it cost him his life. Suddenly, the ragged band of travelers is faced with life on their own. The task of destroying the Ring, which seemed to be an improbability before, looks to be certainly impossible now. Impossible, that is, until an old man crosses their path.

At first, the mysterious old man sends a new wave of panic through the weary fellowship. Legalos, the Elf, draws his bow and prepares for the old: "shoot first and ask questions later" tactic. But he cannot draw a bead. The old man is too fast. He skirts the hills and mountains with confidence, skill, and speed. He is coming right for them and there is nothing they can do but hope he will be on their side. Finally, he is right in front of them, when he does the unthinkable. He engages them in conversation, plain, everyday conversation. Conversation unforced, and calm.

He asks them about their journey. He talks as one who has nothing whatsoever to prove. He moves as one who is unpredictable and free. Who is this man? Is he Saruman, the evil, dark ruler? Is he after the Ring? Is he for them or against them? Who is this man? Finally, the mystery is revealed. Gandolf the Grey is back in town. But he is different. He is stronger. He is astonishingly powerful. He is unattainably glorious. Yet he is with the band of misfits. He eats and drinks with them. He laughs with them. He wants to hear their stories. And more importantly, he tells them his. He died on the bridge of Khazad-Dum, but he defeated death. His glory was veiled at first, and now it is revealed.

5. 1 Cor. 15:20.

This is where the rubber meets the road. What will Gandalf do now? Will he leave the perilous journey to Sam, Frodo, Legalos, and the rest? Are they strong enough to defeat the evil and deadly Saruman as he hunts them? Will Gandalf retire and assume a position next to Yoda and Obi-Wan Kenobi? No. His resurrection is real; his resurrection benefits the company. And he comes back to fight. And he wins battle after battle for a handful of travelers who cannot win on their own.

The resurrected Gandalf is not a disembodied spirit. He is even more powerful and present than before. And his power is used not only for the good of the mission, but for the good of his friends. He wants to spend time with them. He laughs with them. He warns them of upcoming danger and he meets Saruman to do battle on their behalf. The resurrected Gandalf is interested in every step of their journey and he wants to spent time with his friends. Even though he has defeated death, he is still interested in the minutia of everyday life.

In the end, Gandolf, the resurrected wizard looks so much more like he who could help us than Obi-Wan-Kenobi, with his pithy sayings about the Force.

This is what it means to have the resurrected Jesus on our side. He is with us along the journey. He fights for us. His greatness is for us.

And he is so good. He is interested in the day-to-day lives of each of his people. The resurrected Jesus calls us to friendship.

If John's attention to detail proves anything, it is that the resurrected Jesus is intimately involved and interested in the monotony and minutia of our unremarkable lives. In the story of the 153 fish, we see God incarnate, who has just recently taken power over death and left his grave clothes in an empty tomb, sits down to share a meal on the beach with his best friends. He wants to eat and drink with them. Jesus, who was abandoned by these same clowns only days before, simply says, "Breakfast is ready."[6]

This is just a part of the mystery of the resurrection of Jesus: he rose again–fully human–to give us a life of resurrection. And he calls us to the table to hang out with him.

6. Jn. 21:12. (The Message Translation)

13

If Jesus Is For Us, Why Did He Leave?

I WONDER WHAT IT was like for the disciples to hang out with Jesus after he rose from the dead. For Thomas, it was life altering, to see for himself the wounded Christ, and touch his hands and side. For Peter, the meeting was redemptive. Not only was he forgiven three times–one for each denial–but he was sent back into kingdom work three times, as well. Even in his resurrected state, Jesus had not given up on the darkest of doubters. If life was good rolling into Jerusalem with the king riding on the foal of a donkey, life was beyond awesome hanging out with Jesus in his post-resurrected self. What could possibly be next?

In a way it would be like the end of a really good book. The rhythm of the story has taken you up, it has taken you down, it has kept you riveted through what could have been adequate endings. You keep turning pages and cannot believe that there is more. What else could possibly happen? And then you hear the best part. There is a sequel coming out. These last pages are only a setup to something even better.

And the standard for the next installment at this point is pretty high. In the last month and a half, Jesus has been proclaimed king in Jerusalem. He has washed their feet. He has enraged the religious leaders. He has been betrayed, arrested, sentenced, executed, and dead for three days. On the third day, he rose again with power and he appeared to the eleven remaining disciples (Judas is out at this point), and a bunch of other people. Forty days, Jesus is hanging out, doing everything from walking through walls to providing a catch of 153 fish! It has been a hard run being a disciple, these past few years, but now . . . now, anything could happen!

So they ask the question that is on everybody's mind. "Lord, will you at this time restore the kingdom of Israel?"[1] This is the only logical question you can be thinking, as one of the eleven. You have to be thinking that it will get messy around now–but a good kind of messy–messy like a good Clint Eastwood movie. And finally, you are on the right side.

The history of Israel is one of failure after failure. God chooses Abraham but Abraham loses faith. God chooses Jacob but Jacob is a scoundrel. Joseph saves his family but inadvertently leads them into 400 years of slavery. Moses leads the people out of Israel but finds out that wandering in the wilderness is much more terrifying than hunkering down in the safety of slavery. God gives his people judges but they want kings. God gives them a king but he turns against the people. God gives the people David for a king but David's pride leads both indirectly, in the case of his adultery with Bathsheba, and directly, in the case of his God-forbidden census, into a broken kingdom. God gives prophet after prophet, but his people refuse to listen.

Finally, in the person of Jesus, he has spoken a word of righteousness, love, forgiveness, and resurrection. What could possibly come next in the story?

Would Abraham's enemies finally suffer, as has long been promised? Would Jesus wield his newly resurrected body to finally crush all the nations like the clay pots that we are? That is exactly what the disciples were expecting. And who can blame them? "Lord, will you at this time restore the kingdom of Israel?" That sounds like a prayer of eager expectation for holy fire to rain down! Finally, the enemies of God will get their just due. This would seem to be the perfect time to begin the final battle, but Jesus once again, is full of surprises.

---

1. Acts 1:6.

This would have been the opportune time to lay out at least some sort of plan. Jesus has the world at his divine fingertips, his chosen followers at his disposal, and the attention of Jerusalem, a city that was about to host a festival called Pentecost. During this annual national remembrance of God's provision in the wilderness, work was prohibited, and the people lived in tents and ate and drank together. Jesus had been conspicuous at the last Pentecost, publicly inviting people to come and drink his living water![2] If he had garnered attention like that the year before, it was a given that he would use his status as recently crucified and resurrected to steal the show again, right? What was the plan? The disciples seem to be asking the right question.

But for anyone who has spent any time with Jesus, we can attest to the fact that he rarely gives us clear marching orders. And so, in a moment that calls for explanation, Jesus is terse. In a time that calls for clarity, Jesus is confusing. In a time that seems ripe for glory, Jesus deflects attention, first to the Father, then to the Spirit: "it is not for you to know the times or the seasons that the Father has fixed by his own authority. But you will receive power when the Holy Spirit comes upon you, and you will be my witnesses . . ."[3]

In the end, it would not be Jesus who would accomplish the spread of his church. He would leave that up to, of all people, his ignorant, impetuous, doubting, and fair-weather friends. They would be empowered by some mysterious Ghost, and transformed into bold, capable, and faithful messengers of the person and work of Jesus. His plan was jarring, and to be honest, a bit ridiculous.

Then, before Peter had a chance to pull him aside one more time for a good talking to, Jesus was lifted up to heaven, right in front of their eyes. No explanation. No specifics. No pep talk. No question and answer time. Jesus said his peace and ascended back into heaven to sit at the right hand of God the Father Almighty.

After the last night of my job waiting tables, the first time I quit, I was sitting in my favorite bar, trying to make sense out of my life through the power of a cold Guinness. To my right, there was

---

2. Jn. 7:14–24.

3. Acts 1:7–8.

a man who looked just as introspective and gloomy as I am sure I did, so I decided to strike up a conversation. Normally, I am not the type to talk to strangers, an instruction I had received from my mother when I was young, and to date the rule I have kept most religiously over the years. His name was Derrick, and as we started to talk I realized he was in an oddly similar existential quandary as I, although he was nearly twice my age.

We had a drink together, and exchanged stories with one another. I had met a man whose life was falling apart. His wife was leaving him and taking the house. The business he had inherited from his father was going under. As I asked for a second beer, I noticed that his pace was double mine. Our window of opportunity was fading as fast as his sobriety, so I decided to take over the conversation just a little bit. I asked him what he thought of Jesus, and he said he had no idea. Growing up in the South, he knew that there was a church, a gospel, and a bunch of people that dressed up every Sunday, but he said he did not know what it was all about. I started to tell him the story of Jesus.

It was a moment where I look back and know for sure that I needed to hear the story as much as he did. I was about to finish seminary and I had no idea where my life was headed. I had been in love with a girl, and had my heart broken. I was 3,000 miles away from my family. And I had just quit my job. Derrick needed the gospel as much as anybody, but looking back, I'm sure I told him the story for purely mercenary reasons. I needed to hear it.

I told him about creation. God loved himself so much that he rejoiced the world into existence, all things seen and unseen. I told him about Adam and Eve. They were good, but they were weak. I told him about Abraham, Moses, King David, and some of the prophets. We became close enough friends that night to laugh at Ezekiel when he was commanded to eat poop, and we trembled when Isaiah saw the temple of the Lord shaking with glory.

Then I told him about Jesus. I told him about God becoming one of us. I told him about the perfect, law-fulfilling life of God. I told him about Judas, the Pharisees and Pontius Pilate. I told him about Peter and I told him about the cross. Then I told him about Jesus' defeat of death. He was in. He loved the story.

But as I told him about the ascension and his non-reaction told me all I needed to know. As he nodded in polite agreement, I pressed him. "Did you hear what I just said? The story says that once he defeated death, Jesus only spent forty days on earth before he rose up off of the ground and carried himself to the heavenly places." Something about telling this part of the story outside the confines of Sunday morning created an element of comedy, almost. It is surprising. It had to be the last thing the disciples could guess would happen!

And I was comforted once again with the weird plan of God. He displays his victory over death, hell, sin, and the grave by sending down his Spirit to make us new. The divine plan would be translated and spread through a flawed and fearful bunch. Then he would go away and send the unseen Spirit back to them. Nobody saw this coming, which makes it the perfect plot twist.

Sure enough, not long after Jesus promised the Holy Spirit, he came. And he came at Pentecost and spoke through the mouths of retired fishermen and tax collectors. When he came, he turned the whole world upside down.

The ascension marks the new way the message would be made known. We too experience the Almighty through a flawed and fearful people. Our experience of God is now mediated through one another! As we hear the promise of Christ to send his Spirit upon us, we find a new freedom. All of our work from here on out will be a work of rest, a work of faith, and a demonstration of love. In the ascension, Jesus has made known to us that he is not ashamed to use his people to speak his message.

The message today is the same as it was at that second Pentecost, the day the church as born. God is for us. And he has chosen the strangest of messengers to convey what we have come to know as the gospel. He has chosen us. He has chosen very ordinary and very flawed messengers. He has chosen the most fearful among us to speak the message with a boldness that could never arise from us. He has chosen the most fearful among us to deliver the message of the love of God for humanity, knowing full well that love is the most terrifying of adventures. His ascension is a testament to the fact that his appearances today will come through us. Who could see this twist coming?

But his ascension does one more thing. It is a sign that he has power over life as well as death. He did not leave his disciples on the cross, he left them looking up toward the sky, wondering when he would come back. And as they stood there gazing, two men dressed all in white came and posed the second question of the scene, why do you stand here looking into the sky? The type of anticipation this scene gives us is not the stuff of star gazing, but a sort of wonder that mobilizes. It is a sort of wonder that makes us ask what is next?

14

God Became Family

Sometimes I have no idea how Jesus puts up with us. It seems like it would be a whole lot easier for him to bring another gigantic, worldwide flood and start all over again. Sure, he would be breaking his rainbow promise, but then again, if he wiped us all out, who could hold him to it? He would be well within his rights to second guess his decision to spend so much time, energy, and blood over a people suffering from chronic forgetfulness of his promises. Who would hold it against him if he had just the slightest twinge of a divine version of buyer's remorse?

My first big purchase in my life was a department store shirt. I had seen the coolest guy in school wearing a similar version of it around, and I somehow knew that that masterpiece of fabric and buttons was going to put me into the next realm of hipness. Who knows, with the power of that shirt, I might even have the guts to ask out the girl I had had a crush on since grade school. The sky was the limit. But then I saw the price and I did some quick math. The shirt was worth five hours of my minimum wage, but man, it was worth it. I had entered the world of impulse shopping.

I had also entered the world of buyer's remorse, because when I took the shirt home, I put it on and I realized that the shirt added surprisingly little to my overall lot in life. I was still a skinny, pimply twerp, and now I was out forty bucks. I felt like I had been had.

And I felt the same a few years later when I bought my first good writing chair. I was in grad school and I was writing my essays from my perch atop a barstool that I found on clearance at Wal-Mart. I needed a change, needed to move up in the world, and most of all, I needed to save my back from its constant, wrenching pain. So I bought a nice imitation leather desk chair. And there was much rejoicing.

But there was not much money, after I had so improved my life, and I remember sitting on my new chair wondering if I should return it. Did I make a mistake buying a new chair? Was I being too much of a snob not looking for a used chair that had been through previous untold suffering, trials, and tribulations? I was experiencing a return of the case of buyer's remorse.

And I am sure I am not alone. As I look around me, I see a lot of people who seem to have a lot of stuff. Somewhere deep down I bet everybody has some sort of buyer's remorse. I wouldn't blame Jesus for feeling a certain amount of regret for the way things have turned out.

For seven years, I worked in a restaurant, and I would like to share a well-known secret with you. Christians are the worst group of people to wait on. Imagine, if you will, two people walk in and ask for a table for dinner. They smile widely as you greet them, and feign the same type of interest that they have learned in church, listening to a sermon. They amen to your description of the appetizers, and they compliment you on your service. And when it is time for the check, you can only hope that a sinner is paying the bill, because a true Christian is saving the tip money for something really important, something really spiritual, hopefully. Sometimes I get so embarrassed.

Once, a coworker of mine was given—in lieu of money, mind you—a tract explaining to her the way to heaven. The printed propaganda promised that the information found therein was more important than money, and on one hand I had to agree. On the other hand though, outside of giving her an opportunity to let God mysteriously feed her and pay her bills like a modern day Elijah, the tract did nothing to help her right then. How could she hear a gospel of eternal riches when the messengers were not willing to pay their own bills? I wanted to apologize. But more than that, I wanted to run and hide. Who could blame Jesus if he were to drop this whole redemption idea out of sheer shame? Is there an out for him if he develops buyer's remorse? What if Jesus feels like he has been had?

Is Jesus ashamed of our whining? Is he ashamed of our lingering desires to fight God for his throne? Is he ashamed of our unwillingness to help the poor? Is he ashamed of our minds that wander far away from him? Is he ashamed of our fearfulness to donate to his church? In a word, is Jesus ashamed of us? Do we keep him up at night, wondering why he took on the cross for a people who embarrass his name and misrepresent him constantly?

Our hearts would tell us yes. He must be ashamed of our calloused hearts. He must be ashamed of the church's failure to address racism, sexism or genocide. He must be ashamed of our bold tongues and idle hands. But again, we are wrong.

The writer of Hebrews is addressing a group of Jews who had put their faith and trust in Jesus, and they had fallen on hard times. There was a persecution of Jews and Christians alike, and the city of Jerusalem was no longer a safe place to live. If the destruction of the temple in the center of the city had not yet happened, it would soon. The readers had lost property, loved ones, and some of them had, understandably, lost faith. They had embraced the gospel only to turn away at times of trial. Some had developed a strong case of buyer's remorse, and others were afraid of falling into the same traps of fear and despair.

They must have felt defeated. They must have felt like they were trying just to survive the violence around them. They needed to know that Jesus had not abandoned them, even though that must have been the way it seemed. The writer tells them they are not alone, though. "Since the One who saves and those who are saved have a common origin, Jesus doesn't hesitate to treat them as family, saying, 'I'll tell my good friends, my brothers and sisters about you; I'll join them in worship and praise to you.'"[1]

---

1. Heb. 2:11–12. (The Message Translation)

Jesus is not ashamed to call us brothers and sisters. He is not so fickle as to regret his decisions. Redemption was not a decision of impulse, but a story that requires intentionality. Jesus knew what he was getting into from the very beginning, and he, unlike us, has every reason to be proud of each of his choices. But it means much more than that.

If we listen closely, we hear that the writer assumes that the work of Jesus is not over. He did not stop being for us on the cross. He did not stop living for us at the resurrection, and he did not forget about us when he went back into heaven. In fact, Jesus, the firstborn among the brethren, sits at the right hand of the Father and prays for us even now.

In fact, this seems to be driving at the whole point of the story, according to the Apostle Paul. He wrote, "For those whom he foreknew he also predestined to be conformed to the image of his Son, in order that he might be the firstborn among many brothers."[2] This had been the whole plan all along. Jesus would be the eldest brother. He would go first into perfect obedience, first into death, first into resurrection, first into ascension, and first into, according to Paul's word, "glorification." He knew what he was getting into in the first place, since before he laid the foundations of the earth and set it spinning.

Buyer's remorse is not an attribute we can ascribe to the divine. He stands proudly beside a bumbling and embarrassing family. He stands in solidarity with his brothers and sisters who just cannot seem to get it right. He stands as a witness to the Father that we are his daughters and sons, right along with him.

To a people who struggle with fear, with shame, and with seemingly insurmountable obstacles between our current lives and acceptability in the sight of God, Jesus is not ashamed to claim brotherhood, solidarity, and union.

Far from being put off by our constant waywardness, Jesus gathers all of the righteousness at his disposal and presents it to the Father on our behalf. He gives his solidarity freely, as a gift. He does not begrudge his own flesh and blood because he is not waiting

2. Rom. 8:29.

for us to make him look better. He is not worried about us making him look less perfect, spotless, obedient, victorious, or glorious. His confidence is in his own perfection, and he offers the same confidence to his trembling little brothers and sisters.

Our older brother is permanently proud of us.

We have nothing to fear as long as Jesus joins with us. And if he hasn't had enough of us by now, surely there's no end in sight to his patience.

15

Hope and Disappointment

WHEN I WAS YOUNG, I remember staying up late and praying that Jesus did not come back that night. What if I had not figured it all out yet, after all? What if the world ended and I was somewhere between belief and disbelief, like the lukewarm person he promised to spit out of his mouth in the book of Revelation? I was just afraid he would catch me on an off day. Not only that, but I had barely done anything yet! How could he come back and stop time dead in its tracks, forcing me to miss getting my driver's license? Or what if he came back on the day before my first date? I had so much of my life in front of me, how could I hope in his coming again?

And I felt that way right up to the day my favorite baseball player was traded away to Cleveland. Suddenly, something was clearly wrong with the world and it was beyond repair. I feel this disconnect between the way things should be and the way thing are each time I call an eight hundred number and wait for the next representative to assist me. I think my friends feel it when they hang out with me on a day that involves too many details and not enough coffee. Things are not the way they should be and I am not the way I should be. Why does the world spin on as we wait for Jesus to come back and end it all?

I never imagined the return of Jesus as a comforting time. When I was a kid, I was so afraid of being left behind when he came like a thief in the night that I could not think of eternity without fearing that I was going to be on an airplane piloted by a Christian and poof! We were spinning out of control because the guy at the helm taught a Sunday school class. It was all so terrifying.

And as I grew up I began to see that Jesus' promise to come a second time was not only a source of terror, it was also a source of confusion and division. In the nineteenth century, there were some guys who felt so left out of the various gold rushes and wagon trains of the day that they started tracking everything in the Bible that seemed to point to the story of Jesus' return.

Daniel, was discovered, was giving the reader a solid timeline when he talked about a period of seventy weeks and a guy who would be known as the Abomination of Desolation. Likewise, John had apparently written the book of Revelation with the intention of us converting his stories into a chart and placed in a room down the hall from the Sanctuary to be puzzled over each week before the songs started.

Growing up, I was led to believe that the end of the world would be secret, like Jesus' secret middle of the night covert op. Non-believers would wake up in the morning to the utter chaos they have wreaked upon themselves, and like citizens of Gotham City with a broken bat-signal, and they would destroy themselves, in desperation and panic, looking in vain for the Christians. That made sense because who better to turn to in a state of panic than a people who had a stockpile of canned goods in the basement and a chart on the wall predicting the next step?

And to be honest, there is something inside of me that cringes when it is time to talk about God coming back to stop time and institute a new order to things. It may be just me but the whole thing seems really weird. It seems otherworldly. How can we hope in something that we have no concept of? It almost seems like a cruel hope, like telling Chicagoan that the Cubs are finally going to win the World Series this year. And it has only been a little more than century since the Cubs won. It has been two millennia since Jesus left with the promise that he would come back the same way he left us.

One summer I worked at my church, following around the associate pastor. In those three months, I learned that he was in charge of everything from planning the songs each week to cleaning out old ladies' storage units. Oh, and he was in charge of hospital visits.

I always hated the hospital. It smelled so bad and that was the only place I had seen my grandpa without his work boots on. I thought I would never be able to go in there without feeling sick to my stomach. But the first couple of people we visited found their way into the hospital with a high fever or tonsils that needed to be removed, so I started to get the hang of it. I could add that to my list of accomplishments at the tender age of twenty. "Casey Hobbs. Noble visitor of the temporarily hospitalized." That had a pretty good ring to it.

So the day we went in to visit an old woman whose name I have since forgotten, I thought nothing of our drive in. I had, after all, become an expert of sorts, and here was an opportunity to hone my skills. But this visit was different. This woman was dying. And she knew it.

I had wondered from time to time how I would take it if I knew the end was near. I would probably dictate a famous letter or say something profound. Dietrich Bonhoeffer's last words on his way to the gallows, were, "This is the end . . . for me the beginning of life."[1] Bare minimum, I could just repeat those words. But in the back of my mind I was afraid I would go out kicking and screaming. But the dying woman had no visions of grandeur. She just wanted us to read to her.

I will not ever forget the gift that I was given that day, to read the words of the Apostle Paul to a dying woman, "one thing I do: forgetting what lies behind and straining forward to what lies ahead, I press on toward the goal for the prize of the upward call of God in Christ Jesus."[2] I watched as tears rolled down her cheeks. She was so close to the end and she was unafraid. She was about to be free. She

1. Metaxas, *Bonhoeffer*, 528.
2. Phil. 3:13–14.

was about to see God face-to-face. All she had to do was to strain forward for a few more minutes or a few more days.

I realized then that the hope of the coming new creation is for people who are at the edge of death. It is only for those who are willing to press forward for just a little while longer; a few more days, a few more years, a few more decades. To hope in Jesus coming back a second time to restore creation back to the way it was intended to be is only a hope for those who can recognize the discrepancy between the way things are and the way things ought to be.

And I wonder now how sweet those last few days were for her. Her work was nearly done. Her life was spent, no doubt full of fears, full of sins, full of mistakes, but in the end, she had run her race. In the end she could see beauty rising up from the ashes. She could see her Father welcoming her home on the other side of the river. The culmination of her life was within view.

I wonder what my life would look like if I lived it in that sort of mindset. What if, instead of financial security, my hopes lay in the riches of being made a child of God? What if, instead of a life absent of suffering, my hopes lay in a life full of redemption? What if my greatest desire was to see God face-to-face?

This is the culmination of the gospel. If Jesus lived, rejoiced, fulfilled the law, suffered, took on hell, raised himself from the dead, ascended into heaven, took his seat at the right hand of the Father and prayed for us, yet did not come back to redeem his fallen creation, this is all a waste of time. We need him to come back and set the rest of creation right. We need, above anything else, the justice and mercy of God to set everything straight. If we give up hope in the restoration of all things to Christ, we have given up our reason to press on, and to love one another.

Some days I remember what it felt like, you know, that feeling that God is kind of cruel to handle things the way he does, like a dad who promises to throw a ball with his son, but is too busy working to remember his promise. It has been over 2,000 years since we saw him last, and even though he gave us his Spirit to live in us, to mark us, to comfort us, it would be easier to believe it all if we could see him. Enough with this in-between time already! I just get tired of waiting, almost like history has been on hold listening to Muzak for the last twenty centuries.

But Jesus' friend Peter offered a second opinion, for what it is worth. He counted the slowness of God in keeping his promise as a grace all to itself. He wrote: "The Lord is not slow to fulfill his promise as some of you count slowness, but is patient toward you, not wishing that any should perish, but that all should reach repentance."[3] And it is funny, but this only comes as a comfort when our priorities change from getting what we want to start playing our part in the story he is writing. Time marches on as always, with little interruption, and God, with all the patience of a loving father, is waiting for all of his children to come home. And so this in-between time takes on a different character altogether. Today becomes the time of repenting, of turning, of heading home to be forgiven.

But with every day that passes, we are closer to the end. Peter follows up his words about God's patience with a jarring reminder that he is coming, and coming suddenly. Unexpectedly. He will come like a thief in the night.[4] God has not forgotten his promise to take his people home, and he has not forgotten his promise to set all things in heaven and on earth right.

Peter makes a point that the coming end marks a new beginning. "The heavens will pass away with a roar, and the heavenly bodies will be burned up and dissolved, and the earth and the works that are done on it will be exposed."[5] The picture I used to have of the secret, middle of the night, divine covert op does not seem to match up with the one Peter paints. The day of Jesus' return is a day of cosmic upheaval.

In light of the coming upheaval, we might expect Peter to dwell on destruction. He might have reminded the reader of words of Amos, the prophet. "Woe to you who desire the day of the Lord! Why would you have the day of the Lord? It is . . . as if a man fled from a lion, and a bear met him, or went into his house and a

3. 2 Pet. 3:9.
4. 1 Thess. 5:2.
5. 2 Pet. 3:10.

serpent bit him."[6] But the message Peter has for us is not a call to fear, but to freedom. "What sort of people ought you be in lives of holiness and godliness, waiting for and hastening the coming of the day of the Lord . . ."[7] The call is not to live in fear of the end, but in expectancy, a kind of edge of your seat living.

The way we see the end all hinges once again on whether or not we will see the heart of God in his promise to return. Just as he is now waiting for us, he has promised that he is coming back for us. He has not forgotten his promise.

This is a hope that does not disappoint.

And because it doesn't, the world around us is not static. It is humming. It is moving towards a new beginning. In Paul's words, "The created world can hardly wait for what's coming next."[8]

6. Amos 5:18–19.

7. 1 Pet. 3:11–12.

8. Rom. 8:19. (The Message Translation)

16

God's Love for the Unloveable

TWINS SEEM TO HAVE this way of reading each other's thoughts, feeling the other's pain and influencing the other's thinking. Some twins grow to hate each other and some grow to be joined at the hip, even to old age. There is a special bond that twins share with one another. But familiarity can breed contempt just as well.

I grew up playing ball with a pair of twins who were my own age and there was a time when they were inseparable. They cared about one another. They played with one another. They defended one another. They had fun as a team. But then something happened. Somewhere along the way, they had enough of one another. But they still could not escape the fact that people saw them as one person. They ended up hating one another.

I understand because I also have a twin brother. As close as we were growing up, rivalry has always been a part of our story. For instance, Jay was always stronger than I was. He would be out back and chopping wood for the fire with dad while I was inside with mom setting the table for dinner. Jay decided to join the wrestling team in the sixth grade. I opted to stick to my rule of staying out of sweaty, smelly rooms. Jay has always been the one to camp, fish and hunt. My stories associated with any of the three include my dropping my fishing pole in a river and running from unseen wildlife.

On the other hand, I was naturally more athletic than my brother. Of course, that discrepancy was eliminated early on, when

Jay worked twice as hard as I did to learn to field a ground ball. Jay (All ninety pounds of him) was the starting catcher on our varsity baseball team when we were freshmen in high school. I got to work on my sunflower seed distance spitting abilities in my many hours on the bench.

Some twins take these differences in stride and others build up a ton of resentment for each other. This was the case in the Old Testament story of Jacob and Esau.

Now, I think it is worth pointing out that most people view brothers who are born at the same time as one person. My dad had a friend who for years had assumed he had a son named "JayandCasey." "JayandCasey have a ballgame today," dad would say. "JayandCasey are headed to the prom." It was years before, after hearing a story about me that did not include Jay, his friend discovered his ignorance. "Wait—who is Casey?"

Being a twin has always had its own perks, but the downside is the fight for your own identity. So it makes sense that Jacob and Esau, the biblical twins, struggled with their own identities. Theirs is a story of rivalry, cheating, lying, and overall dysfunction. And Jacob, as it turned out, was at the bottom of most of it.

Esau learned the hard way that if you have your identity attached with another person you better hope they are pretty loveable.

Jacob was a classic mammas boy, while Esau, the oldest, was a rough-and-tumble hunter, a man's man. And more importantly, Esau was his father Isaac's favorite. Jacob, who would become the main character, was anything but loveable. Yet, God loved him before he was born. He chose him to be the favored twin. He chose him to keep his grandfather Abraham's promise alive. If you know the story, you may know why I have a bit of an issue with God's choice.

Jacob lived up to his name, which meant: "liar," or, "schemer." He was the type of guy who would look you in the eyes and shake your hand right before he stabbed you in the back. Jacob was not the kind of guy you would be proud to be associated with at all. If you think you are unloveable–maybe that you have somehow disqualified yourself from the love of God–just consider three episodes in Jacob's life that jump to mind.

"One day Jacob was cooking a stew. Esau came in from the field, starved. Esau said to Jacob, 'Give me some of that red stew—I'm starved!' That's how he came to be called Edom (Red).

Jacob said, 'Make me a trade: my stew for your rights as the firstborn.'

Esau said, 'I'm starving! What good is a birthright if I'm dead?'

Jacob said, 'First, swear to me.' And he did it. On oath Esau traded away his rights as the firstborn. Jacob gave him bread and the stew of lentils. He ate and drank, got up and left. That's how Esau shrugged off his rights as the firstborn."[1]

Ok, granted, this story is about Esau's disregard for God's blessing in his life. That is why Esau is known for having: "shrugged off his birthright." The main point is that Esau could really care less about God's rule and reign. He wanted momentary pleasure and relief more than he wanted to wait for God to provide for him. We have all been in the same spot as Esau.

But as much as I know this is the main point (and it is), I have a hard time ignoring the fact that Jacob was so cruel, heartless and cold as to bribe him of something so important! In that move, Jacob, in effect, took everything from Esau. He lost the blessing of his father (Esau, remember, had always been his dad's favorite). He lost the financial opportunity he had as his natural right, being—if only slightly—older than Jacob. Now Jacob would get the larger share of the family wealth.

The worst part was that Esau pretty much slapped God in the face. And his brother Jacob was right there to make sure he fell face-down in the mud.

Can you imagine how dirty and low-down Jacob must have felt in the depths of his soul? How could God ever forgive him for overseeing the failure of his brother? That kind of disregard for his brother is despicable. What kind of man clicks his heels at the destruction of his own flesh and blood?

I can tell you that is a guy who nobody I would ever want to be seen with, let alone embrace.

---

1. Gen. 25:29–34 (The Message Translation)

To make matters worse, Jacob stole his brother's inheritance and blessing. Again. No, this is not the same story. Jacob stole his brother's inheritance two times![2] And if you think the first time was bad, consider that the second time, Jacob teamed up with his own mother to deceive his dad and cheat his brother. We get the idea that biblical characters are known for their purity, piety, and holiness. Jacob and his mom were just lucky Jerry Springer would not be on the air for another couple of thousand years. They put the "fun" back in "dysfunctional!"

This morbidly fascinating tale has Isaac, Jacob's dad, as an old man. He is blind and he is dying, so he calls in his eldest, and favorite son, Esau. Even though Esau had caused the family some grief by marrying a Hittite (which is always a bad call), Isaac still wanted to give him his rightful blessing, so he sent him out to the wilderness to kill some game and make him some stew. Perhaps Esau thought that the second episode of hunting for soup would turn out better than the first. And so Esau goes out to hunt.

So what do Jacob and his mom do? Spend some good, quality time with the old man, right? Wrong. Clean up the kitchen so it will be easy for Esau to cook his game? Nope. Did the schemers decide to mind their own respective businesses and let this golden opportunity pass them by? Yeah right. How about tricking the old man? Now we are on to something.

So Jacob kills a goat, cooks it up and gets ready to serve it to the blind old man. Just one more detail: time to tie some of the goatskin around Jacob's silky-smooth arms to make him appear as manly as Esau.

And, long story short, it worked. Jacob got the whole blessing that Esau had coming. Esau gets to wander around like a prisoner on the lam. Once again Jacob has slithered around and ruined Esau's life over a bowl of soup.

Can you imagine being Jacob? You just have to feel like your soul is as dark as coal. Nobody could ever love a man who was so crooked as to steal a blessing from his own father! And what about this holy, wrathful God of justice of whom your dad has always

2. Gen. 27:1–46.

spoken? How could he ever accept such a wicked schemer? Even if you measure sin on a sliding scale this one tips it.

But there is one more sordid scene that comes to mind with Jacob.

Jacob is perhaps best known for his night of wrestling with God. He had come to a point in his life that he finally had an encounter with the God of his fathers, and this is the turning point in his life:

"The man said, 'Let me go; it's daybreak.' Jacob said, 'I'm not letting you go 'til you bless me.'

The man said, 'What's your name?' He answered, 'Jacob.'

The man said, 'But no longer. Your name is no longer Jacob. From now on it's Israel (God-Wrestler); you've wrestled with God and you've come through.'

Jacob asked, 'And what's your name?' The man said, 'Why do you want to know my name?' And then, right then and there, he blessed him. Jacob named the place Peniel (God's Face) because, he said, 'I saw God face-to-face and lived to tell the story!'"[3]

Jacob's identity was changed. No longer is he known by his old name. His old fused identity with Esau was a thing of the past. He had a true encounter with God and he was a new man. His name is no longer: "Schemer" but, "God-Wrestler." His life was changed forever. And he went out the next day to meet his brother for the first time in nearly twenty years. And do you know what he did? Jacob bribed his brother with his own family.

Jacob had run for his life after stealing Esau's blessing and settled down with a family of his own. When their paths finally cross, even after this life-altering encounter with God, Jacob is still not bold enough to go out and face him. The great Jacob elects to send his entire family out in front of him. And who better to meet your bloodthirsty brother after all those years than your wife and kids?

Seriously, have you ever seen such a weasel? To call Jacob a schemer or a liar seems like the greatest of understatements. He personified lying. He is the king of the schemers. He lied to his brother, stole sheep from his father-in-law, and he scammed his

---

3. Gen. 32:35–32. (The Message Translation)

father. Later on in the story, in an un-Esau-related moment, Jacob's embarrassing favoritism of his second-youngest son, Joseph, led directly to four hundred years of slavery in Egypt. "Jacob, the Schemer." That's like "Michael Jordan the Basketball Player," "Tiger Woods the Golfer," "Thomas Edison the Inventor." Jacob was not just a schemer. He was the coupe de grace of all schemers. Jacob is the ultimate schemer, even the day after his dramatic night of wrestling God.

On the flip side, what did Esau do? He had it in his power the whole time to wipe Jacob off the face of the earth. Jacob was a momma's boy and Esau was a country boy that would put Hank Williams Jr. to shame. Jacob's mom favored him because he could cook up a mean lintel soup; Esau's dad favored him because he was the quintessential man's man.

And how did Esau respond to Jacob's lifetime of schemes, manipulation, coercion, and lies? "But Esau ran up and embraced him, held him tight and kissed him"[4] You can almost see Esau as the forerunner to the father in Jesus' parable of the prodigal, who did his share of embracing, weeping, and kissing over being reunited with his scheming son.[5] In the story of the Bible, his forgiveness is on a short list.

You see, his actions were consistently flawless. He does all the things a forgiving person is supposed to do over and over again. He does all the things a good, upright, honest God-fearing person should do and yet he is passed over by God.

This is why it is a shock to hear the prophet Malachi's words echoed by the Apostle Paul, "God hated Esau."[6]

As many times as I have read about Jacob and Esau, I still cannot believe that this is the conclusion to the matter. It almost seems as if God himself would be moved to respect and appreciation for somebody who does all the right things (they seem to be a pretty rare group, after all!). And once again it is apparent that God is playing by his own set of rules.

---

4. Gen. 33:4. (The Message Translation)
5. Lk.15:20.
6. Mal. 1:2; Rom. 9:13.

God has long been in the business of loving the unlovable and passing over the good, decent, and acceptable. He was in no way surprised that Jacob would be a schemer and Esau would be a forgiving and overall, swell guy. Yet, he chose Jacob and loved him before he made the world and started spinning it on its axis. Likewise, he decided he would pass over Esau, leaving him to his respectable and good-natured self.

What at first seems like a miscarriage of justice make sense if you take a longer look at Esau. At the end of the day, Esau never seemed to believe that he needed God. His own goodness is what kept him from calling upon the Lord, and stuck in a cycle of self-congratulation, Esau ended up in isolation and separation from God. Far from being on his side, God was against Esau

And you know what else? He is against Esau and his descendents still. This is what James, the brother of Jesus, meant when he said, "God opposes the proud?"[7] God does not call us to be respectable. He does not call us to be–in and of ourselves–good people. He calls us to be humble.

Though he never seemed to get it right, Jacob's name was nevertheless changed to Israel. His identity changed. Jacob had contended with God and God had won. It would take Jacob the rest of his life to live out this change, but still God never gave up on him.

And the Lord is still in this business, of loving the unlovable while utterly rejecting the nicest of folks. He seems to go out of his way to set his love on the most unlikely scoundrels.

This is why Jesus is not ashamed to call all of us Jacobs into his family. He loves the most flawed. He loves the ones who have made a habit of deceit. He loves hotheads. He loves cheaters. He loves liars. He loves addicts. And our most dramatic sins can do nothing to stop his pursuit.

This is the great, unforeseen, and perfect twist in the gospel. God is not afraid to attach himself to us. Jesus identifies himself with a bunch of Jacobs. He is not ashamed of us. He is not ashamed to be near us. He does not regret his decision to love us. The story of the love of God for schemers goes deeper still.

7. Jas. 4:6.

He also identifies us. He calls us by his own name. He gives us his own goodness. He gives us his own obedience. He gives us his own love. He gives us his own passion for justice. He gives us his own patience, kindness, goodness, gentleness, and self-control. He gives us his own wholeness. Who could see that coming?

And are you now afraid to mess this whole plan up? Are you really strong enough to throw a wrench into God's intentions? If he has loved you before he created the world,[8] he will love you even after you have thrown your life in the proverbial ditch.

God has a long, documented history of loving the unloveable.

That God is confronting us with his goodness day after day would be good news whether we deserved it or not. We could all use the pursuing compassion of the God of the universe. And there may be some people out there who are more deserving of God's compassion than the rest of us. But for me, I can't help but see more of myself in Jacob than I would like to admit. I suspect that I am not alone.

From beginning to end, the story of God is the story of Jesus loving the unloveable. One mishap after another could no more disqualify Jacob from God's compassion than Esau's self-righteousness could impress the Almighty.

Are you afraid of yourself? Are you afraid that you'll be disqualified from the pursuit of God because of your past? Are you afraid of blowing it in the future? Take a lesson from Jacob. God loves the unloveable.

And he loves us enough to change us.

---

8. Eph. 1:4.

17

Joining Together Head and Heart

"It is not excess of thought but defect of fertile and generous emotions that marks (us) out. (Our) heads are no bigger than ordinary: it is the atrophy of the chest beneath that makes (us) seem so."[1]

Years ago, C.S. Lewis pointed out a trend that he referred to as the "abolition of man." He had stumbled upon a grammar book about poetry that had become standard in the school systems. The authors of the book had set out to teach children the difference between objective reality and subjective feelings, in order to "enlighten" grade-schoolers. Lewis was not a fan.

He pointed out their handling of a poem by William Wordsworth, upon seeing a waterfall. The poet described the scene as "sublime." Whether it was the cascading young snow runoff against ancient stones, the glory of the sunshine hitting the water at a certain angle or the constant downhill rumble, Wordsworth felt he could use the word sublime. I think each of us was subjected to some similar grammar that Lewis was reading from, because their first move was to scrutinize the poet. Had Wordsworth really meant that the waterfall was, in itself, sublime? Was the waterfall not, after all, a common phenomenon of melting snow heading toward the ocean? The scene, pointed out

---

1. Lewis, *The Abolition of Man*, 25.

the academic geniuses, was ordinary. Wordsworth was describing his own feelings. Lewis hated this line of reasoning.

The grammar book was teaching, in the subtlest of ways, that it is more important to observe than to feel. They operated under the assumption that feelings are unimportant; only what can be touched, seen, tasted, heard, or smelled was real. The next step is to say that our feelings have less importance than our five senses.

We have grown up being taught the same ideas. Our feelings are in the way of our growth as women and men, so we ignore them, cast them aside, and work to achieve enough success to stifle the voice of fear we cannot seem to shake.

What happens along the way, Lewis said, was this atrophy of the heart. Our desires shrink. Our fears, un-confronted, drive us into a state of paralysis. Our lives stagnate. We choose comfort over freedom and we are lulled to sleep by a devil who is more real than we give him credit for. Our lives are, at best, dutiful; and at worst, ineffective, unloving, and callous. Our heads have been divorced from our hearts and we have become these men and women without chests. We have become the generation of lost boys and girls.

Our unwillingness to grow up is no more evident than in our most central tasks as women and men made in the image of God. Somebody once asked Jesus to sum up the entirety of the purpose of humanity and he did it with one command and two recipients. The command is to love. The recipients are God and neighbor. Simple enough. Love God, love neighbor.[2] Usually, I think I pretty much rule at the first and get a passing grade in the second. Usually I am wrong.

The Heidelberg Catechism gets it right though. After establishing that Jesus' summation of the law is our requirement before God, the question is asked, "Can you live up to all this perfectly?"[3] The answer gets right to the point. "No." Pretty harsh, but there is more. "I have a natural tendency to hate God and my neighbor." You have to love how they used to get right to the point. We only

---

2. Matt. 22:37–40.

3. DeYoung, *The Good News We Almost Forgot*, 24.

have one rule, when you get down to it, and it is love. The problem is that we are abysmal when it comes to love.

On April 3 1968, in the midst of the strike of sanitation workers who were getting unfair wages and treatment, Dr. Martin Luther King Jr. retold Jesus' story of the Good Samaritan. The story is about a man who is beaten and left for dead on the side of the road leading to Jericho. Two respectable, holy men walked right past him, lying in a pool of his own blood.

How could two men who were servants of God and neighbor turn a blind eye to a man in need? Were they in a hurry, as Dr. King suggested, making it just on time to the Jericho Road Improvement Association? Did they see him as just another number of a growing disenfranchised community? Perhaps, but Dr. King suggested another reason. They were afraid. As much as the religious leaders preached about love, they were unwilling to get their hands dirty and take a risk. Dr. King suggested an explanation that hits all-too close to home.

He said, "And so the first question that the priest asked–the first question that the Levite asked was, "If I stop to help this man, what will happen to me?"[4]

Do you hear yourself in that? Just like children, their first thought is for their own safety. What will happen if we stop to help a stranger? What if this is a trap and the man is only faking it to get our sympathy and money? What if he is violent? After all, priests and Levites are not known for their street-fighting abilities. Then what will happen to our people, who need our pastoral advice and intervention? No, we will have to risk too much.

In the end, the two holy men decided that stopping to help one dying man on the street was not worth the risk to their personal safety, comfort, righteousness, or reputation. They opted for the easy way out and it nearly cost the dying man his life. And do you know what else? They would have never known how much it cost him. How could they? Their focus was not on helping a stranger. It was about preserving and saving their respective respectable skins. We have a word for this type of behavior. It is called selfishness.

4. King, *Martin Luther King Jr.'s Biblical Epic*, 117.

Whatever the excuse, the story boils down to two good men who were not interested in helping a man in distress. They were like children: selfish and fearful.

And I wish I could say I was more like the Good Samaritan at the end of the story, but I can relate with the first two much more. When I have been called to have faith like a child, I find I only have the focus of one. The question echoes deep down. I hear it when I pass by homeless men and women on the streets of Seattle. I hear it each time a friend is in crisis. I'd like to help, but the question lingers in the back of my mind, "What will happen to me?"

This is the question of a child, not of a man, or of a woman. This is the question of a slave, not someone who is free. It is the question of a coward, not a lover.

I am so thankful that I am not alone. There are men and women who have had courage enough to become great lovers, in spite of the greatest of odds.

Dietrich Bonhoeffer was born the son of an affluent German professor of psychiatry and neurology in 1906. During his childhood, his brother, Hans, was a casualty of World War I, and by the time he was an adult, the people of Germany were just about to begin their love affair with Adolf Hitler. As Hitler took power in 1933, Bonhoeffer was among the first voices of opposition to the "Third Reich." A lover of his country, Dietrich Bonhoeffer's first citizenship was of the kingdom of God and he recognized that Hitler's thirst for power set himself as blatant enemy of the church.

At the start of World War II, Dietrich Bonhoeffer had it made. His father was a respected and influential man. Of course, nobody could opt out of war completely at that time, but he could have flown right under the radar as a chaplain in the service, awaiting the day he could be free from the memories of war. An older and wiser theologian named Karl Barth, a Swiss opponent of Hitler, pleaded for him to escape Germany. He even took a trip to New York City, having been coaxed to step out of harms' way by friends. He could have written strongly against the oppression of his nation's leaders from a safe distance.

But Bonhoeffer was, as Lewis would have said, "a man with a chest." We might just say that he had courage in the face of danger;

he could not stomach the idea of a life of cowardice. He quickly returned to Germany, and back into harm's way after only a month in the States. The War was only just beginning and Bonhoeffer would spend the remaining seven years of his life speaking, writing, and even participating in the plot that nearly assassinated The Fuhrer from the most dangerous of places for an opponent of the Third Reich: Berlin.

His friend Helmut Traub remembered Dietrich Bonhoeffer's surprise return to Germany: "I was immediately up in arms, blurting out how he could come back after it cost us so much trouble to get him into safety–safety for us, for our cause, here everything was lost anyway. He very calmly lit a cigarette. Then he said he had made a mistake in going to America . . . he knew he had taken a clear step (in returning to Germany), though the actualities before him were still unclear."[5]

What would possess Bonhoeffer to return? The answer is simple. His head and his heart were in line with each other. The call of God on his life was to love the people in his homeland, even if that would cause his safety, and ultimately his life. Love drove him into the fray, beyond his fear and into a freedom that allowed him to love and value others over himself.

As inspiring as the story of Bonhoeffer is, sometimes I miss the message of his life. Here was a man in the most dramatic of circumstances. He stood up against Nazis. He was a pacifist who was executed for trying to assassinate Adolf Hitler. He was the leader of an underground seminary. He wrote passionate and profound letters from prison toward the end of his life that speak to millions to this day. Bonhoeffer put his life on the line for the sake of love and most of us will never know what that feels like. We are not all called to such a dramatic sacrifice.

But Christ is calling each of us to be the women and men we are made to be. Some of us will be thrust into these once in a generation decisions, but most of us are being called to live, in the

---

5. Metaxas, *Bonhoeffer*, 345.

words of Bonhoeffer, lives of: "simple, unreflecting obedience to the will of Christ."[6]

Our stories are mundane. They are common. They are ordinary. Nobody writes books or makes movies about a guy who goes to work on time every day and provides for his family, but most of us are called to do just that. We may have our moments in the sun but those times are fleeting. Soon enough, our accomplishments become unknown and obscure. The question to us becomes: "how will I live joyfully, faithfully, and courageously into the common life God has called me to?"

The call on our lives is the same whether we are famous or obscure. We are called to be nothing more or less than the men and women we were made to be. We are called to unite our head and a heart in love for God and love for others. It sounds really simple on paper.

But we have the same struggles that Lewis pointed out in *The Abolition of Man*. We have an atrophy of the heart. We are cowards, all. Well, at least I am.

And how can I expect to have pity on others when I am full of self-pity? How can my heart be whole if I am unwilling to experience fear, as well as joy? How can I care for others when I am so consumed by what they will think of me? My every instinct rages against becoming this type of a person. But I know I am not alone.

Even Bonhoeffer, who was bold enough to place himself in harm's way and sacrifice his life in the name of love, struggled with the same fears I know so well. As he sat in a prison cell awaiting his execution, not too long after his bold and irreversible decision to return to Berlin and join in the conspiracy against Hitler, Bonhoeffer struggled with self-pity and doubt. He wondered if his life was a sham. He feared he was giving his life for no reason.

At the depths of his despair, he clung to the truth that sustained him. Waiting in a prison camp in Tegel, with his death growing near, Bonhoeffer penned a poem. He wrote:

"Who am I? This man today and tomorrow another?
Am I both at once? An imposter to others,

---

6. Bonhoeffer, *The Cost of Discipleship*, 153.

but to me little more than a whining, despicable weakling?
Does what is in me compare to a vanquished army,
That flees in disorder before a battle already won?
Who am I? They mock me those lonely questions of mine,
Whoever I am, you know me, O God. You know I am yours."[7]

The faith that a young theologian proposed years earlier was what brought him through the darkest night of his soul. God was for him.

And he is for us, too. He comes after us with his love, even when we are at the end of our ropes. A life of courage may end prematurely. Living with head and heart united will lead us into a whole world of danger we could otherwise avoid. And there's no guarantee we'll feel great about the experience. So why do we pursue freedom? Why do we want to be courageous?

Could there be a hint of the image of God still holding on within us, aching to be discovered?

---

7. Bonhoeffer, *A Testament to Freedom*, 514.

18

The God Who Is For Us

WHEN WE TALK ABOUT freedom, what are we getting at? Do we want to be free from the consequences of our actions? Do we want to be free from the responsibilities that life entails? Do we want liberation from the rule of God in our lives? Do we want freedom from fear?

You might have guessed it by now, but the message of this book couldn't be further away from that "cheap freedom." Nowhere in the Bible are we promised a life free from the consequences of Adam and Eve's decision to usurp the role of the Living God in their lives. We are still reaping a harvest that is littered with the fruit that spoiled that day in a Garden so many years ago. And promising each other freedom from pain, freedom from the hurt that we cause ourselves and each other, or freedom from living with the consequences of our self-focused lives is offering false hope. And it has nothing to do with the gospel.

But it sure sounds good.

Before we were married, I went to change the oil in my wife's–then girlfriend's–car. At the time, she lived with a family that was in to growing their own vegetables, fruit, and even raising their own chickens. They had a little urban farm going on and it was awesome. But I had to change the oil. And I did a lousy job.

Unfortunately, I have done several lousy jobs changing the oil in my wife's car, so I'll be more specific.

This time, everything seemed to go smoothly. I had the right tools, I had all afternoon, and the sun was shining. Conditions were perfect. I was so excited that I had even decided to change the oil in my truck at the same time. After I breezed through her car, I strolled triumphantly over to my truck, only to realize that the guy at the parts store had given me the wrong oil filter. Out of nowhere, I was blind with rage.

I know, it's hard to explain why something so simple would move me from triumph to rage in such a short amount of time, but then again, I was working on cars, so on the way to return the part, I felt entitled to shout some words that are best off forgotten.

But I had already taken apart the truck, so I decided to take the car I had already fixed. But there was a problem. I hadn't screwed in the oil filter well enough. Unbeknownst to me, as I drove away, I left a pool of oil on the driveway, right next to a planter-box full of kale.

To make a long story short and to save myself the embarrassment of including too many details, I'll just say the next couple of months were full of searching for solutions for the mess I had put myself in. I had to figure out a way to soak the oil off the driveway. Then I had to figure out how to fix the car I had inadvertently destroyed. Later, I found myself struggling with how I would break the news to my wife that I had caused irreparable damage to her car.

I can't count the amount of times throughout those months that I swung back and forth on the continuum of false hope and despair. One day I was sure I could rebuild the engine. The next, I was sure I had ruined everything from the driveway to the kale to my relationship with my wife in that moment of anger. I was desperate to find a way out of the trouble I had caused.

We want solutions to the mess we are in. And sometimes it doesn't matter how crazy the plan sounds, if it offers relief, we'll give it a shot. And self-help gurus disguised as pastors are more than happy to offer slipshod plans of escape every Sunday. Just like the false prophets of Jeremiah's day, they offer to heal our wounds proclaiming, "Peace! Peace! When there is no peace."[1] But in the end, the healing is light, temporary, and only leads us to lose faith that

---

1. Jer. 6:14.

there remains any true healing from our pain, from the wounds we have caused, and from our debilitating fear of what will come. We need more than a solution to the mess we are in. We need salvation from it.

And isn't it at least ironic that, in expecting salvation from God, it is oftentimes his greatness–the evidence of his strength to help us–that scares us away? We reconstruct God–embracing his goodness perhaps–in our own image. But the god we have made is not strong enough to help us.

Our pet version of the Father is not powerful enough to cause us to tremble. Our preferred version of Jesus is not perplexing enough to stop us dead in our tracks, to cause us to wait for his healing. And our vision of the Holy Spirit receives, at best, lip service. This reconstructed Spirit is not wild enough to move freely through the landscape of our lives.

Is it any wonder, then, that the goodness of God seems almost trivial? What comfort is it to us when he speaks to Jeremiah, saying, "I will plant them in this land . . . with all my heart and all my soul,"[2] when we refuse to let him put his fear into our hearts?

The only way we can be changed by God is to encounter him. We have to sit with him. We have to let him disturb us a little. We have to let him be as great as he is, if we want his goodness to mean anything to us. And when we start to get a picture of the greatness of God, it makes his goodness more refreshing than we thought possible.

The freedom that God offers in Jesus is a costly freedom. It is a freedom that cost not only Jesus' life; it is also a freedom that requires us to surrender our lives to him. And this is not a freedom that is intended to leave us alone, but one that connects us to God and to one another. And this is a freedom that is much powerful than simply a ticket out of our mess. This is a freedom that allows us to do what we never could hope to do before. This is a freedom that allows us to be remade into a people who love.

As the Apostle John wrote, "This is how we've come to understand and experience love: Christ sacrificed his life for us. This is

2. Jer. 32:41.

why we ought to live sacrificially for our fellow believers, and not just be out for ourselves."[3]

This life of love will look different for each of us. Some of us will be transformed in what seems like moments, like Paul on the road to Emmaus, when he met Jesus for the first time.[4] But for the rest of us, we will likely identify more with Peter and with Jacob. Minutes after our greatest moments of faith, we find ourselves cowering in fear.

The message of God is the same to us as it has been all along. The message he promised long ago through the prophets. The message he proved through his incarnation, perfect life, suffering, death, and descent into hell. It is the same message he guaranteed through his resurrection, left us with in his ascension, and continues on in his life before God for us. It is the same message that he will bring with him when he returns to call his people back again. And it is the same message that is ours no matter how far we have fallen. The message:

God is for us.

3. 1 Jn. 3:16–17. (The Message Translation)
4. Acts 9:1–18.

Bibliography

St. Athanasisus. *On the Incarnation*. St. Vladimir's Seminary Press: Crestwood, New York, 1998.

Berry, W. Grinton. *Foxe's Book of Martyrs*. Grand Rapids: Baker, 2001.

Bonhoeffer, Deitrich. *Christ the Center*. San Francisco: Harper-Collins, 1978.

———. *The Cost of Discipleship*. New York: Touchstone, 1995.

———. *Ethics*. New York: MacMillan, 1978.

———. *A Testament to Freedom: The Essential Writings of Dietrich Bonhoeffer*. San Francisco: HarperCollins, 1995.

Calvin, John. *Institutes of the Christian Religion: Book I*. Grand Rapids: Eerdmans, 1995.

DeYoung, Kevin. *The Good News We Almost Forgot*. Chicago: Moody, 2010.

Dylan, Bob. *I Want You* from *Blonde on Blonde*: New York: Columbia Records, 1966. Digital Release 2004.

Kierkegaard, Søren. In Orbis Books, *Bread and Wine*. Farmington, PA: Plough Publishing, 2003.

King, Martin Luther, Jr. In Keith Miller, *Martin Luther King Jr's Biblical Epic*. Jackson: University of Misssissippi. 2011.

Lewis, C.S. *The Abolition of Man*. San Francisco: HarperOne, 2001.

———. *The Chronicles of Narnia*. San Francisco: Harper-Collins, 2001.

Lieth, John. *Creeds and Confessions*. Louisville: Westminster John Knox Press, 1982.

Luther, Martin. In Fredrich Bente, *Historical Introductions to the Book of Concord*. St. Louis: Concordia.

Metaxas, Eric. *Bonhoeffer: Pastor, Martyr, Prophet, Spy*. Nashville: Thomas Nelson, 2010.

Portis, Clinton. *True Grit*. New York: Overlook, 2010.

Steinbeck, John. *The Grapes of Wrath*. New York: Penguin Books, 1999.

Steanger Than Fiction. Directed by Marc Forester. 2006. Culver City, CA: Columbia Pictures, 2006. DVD.